the technology coordinator's handbook

Max Frazier
Gerald D. Bailey

International Society for Technology in Education
EUGENE, OREGON • WASHINGTON, DC

The Technology Coordinator's Handbook

Max Frazier and Gerald D. Bailey

Director of Publishing Jean Marie Hall	Copy Editor Nancy Olson
Acquisitions Editor Scott Harter	Book Design Kim McGovern
Production Editor Tracy Cozzens	Cover Design Kim McGovern
Production Coordinator Amy Miller	Layout and Production Kim McGovern

International Society for Technology in Education (ISTE)
Washington, DC, Office:
    1710 Rhode Island Ave. NW, Suite 900, Washington, DC 20036-3132
Eugene, Oregon, Office:
    180 West 8th Ave., Suite 300, Eugene, OR 97401-2916
Order Desk: 1.800.336.5191
Order Fax: 1.541.302.3778
Customer Service: orders@iste.org
Book Publishing: books@iste.org
Rights and Permissions: permissions@iste.org
Web: www.iste.org

First Edition
ISBN 978-1-56484-211-4

Printed in the United States of America

About ISTE

The International Society for Technology in Education (ISTE) is the trusted source for professional development, knowledge generation, advocacy, and leadership for innovation. A nonprofit membership association, ISTE provides leadership and service to improve teaching, learning, and school leadership by advancing the effective use of technology in PK–12 and teacher education.

Home of the National Educational Technology Standards (NETS), the Center for Applied Research in Educational Technology (CARET), and the National Educational Computing Conference (NECC), ISTE represents more than 85,000 professionals worldwide. We support our members with information, networking opportunities, and guidance as they face the challenge of transforming education. To find out more about these and other ISTE initiatives, visit our Web site at **www.iste.org**.

As part of our mission, ISTE Book Publishing works with experienced educators to develop and produce practical resources for classroom teachers, teacher educators, and technology leaders. Every manuscript we select for publication is carefully peer-reviewed and professionally edited. We look for content that emphasizes the effective use of technology where it can make a difference—increasing the productivity of teachers and administrators; helping students with unique learning styles, abilities, or backgrounds; collecting and using data for decision making at the school and district levels; and creating dynamic, project-based learning environments that engage 21st-century learners. We value your feedback on this book and other ISTE products. E-mail us at **books@iste.org**.

Contents

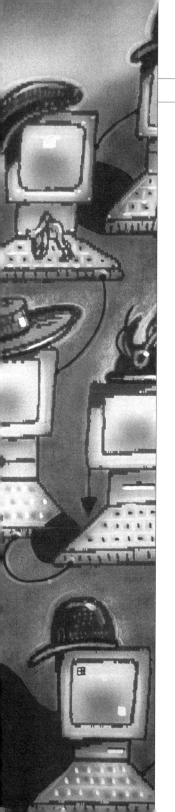

a position without a protocol

the technology coordinator position is relatively new to K–12 schools. The position first appeared in the 1980s when schools began to use computers in day-to-day instruction (Moursund, 1992). As the number of computers rapidly increased, it became obvious to administrators that additional support was needed to manage this new educational technology. Funding a technology coordinator position was a first step toward creating the specialized support staff many larger schools and districts now require to assist with the implementation of both instructional technology in classrooms and administrative technology in school offices.

Teaching and learning are at the heart of all educational organizations, and they must be a primary focus of the technology coordinator. The coordinator will need to work with both teaching and administrative staff to select and purchase appropriate electronic instructional resources for use in the classroom and then help teachers understand and use these new and exciting resources. The coordinator will be responsible for collecting and sharing information with staff regarding current research and best practices. By effectively managing these electronic instructional resources for the school or district, the technology coordinator can have a direct impact on student learning.

Providing end users with technical support is an important responsibility of the technology coordinator. Any organization that hopes to use technology successfully must be prepared to provide users of that technology with all the support and assistance necessary, working with them to diagnose and solve problems that can frustrate and compromise their ability to work. The tech coordinator must help minimize user frustration by establishing effective procedures for providing timely assistance and creating a system for reporting, documenting, and repairing equipment.

The technology coordinator is also responsible for ensuring that software licenses and installations are up to date and that appropriate network and desktop protection software is installed to defend against viruses and worms. The tech coordinator must work with school or district administrators to create a plan and procedure for the regular upgrade and replacement of technology resources. By successfully addressing each of these issues, the coordinator can ensure that end users will be able to take advantage of their school's or district's technology with a minimum of frustration and difficulty.

The school or district network plays a vital part in connecting classrooms, offices, and support services for purposes of communication, data storage, and sharing of information. Consequently, the technology coordinator must be prepared to play a role in planning, implementing, and supporting network operations to ensure the school or district has the infrastructure necessary to achieve the goals of its technology plan. The coordinator works closely with network administrators to manage user accounts, maintain and support the district e-mail system, provide Internet access, and train users to use these resources appropriately. By successfully carrying out this role, the technology coordinator can help ensure that the network will operate smoothly and with a minimum amount of downtime, and that users will gain the maximum utility from available resources.

Another major role technology coordinators typically play is overseeing the administrative computing operations of the school or district. A successful school organization must be able to plan, implement, and manage a variety of database structures to support processing of student grades, human resources information, purchasing, and other information needed by management. The tech coordinator should be prepared to assist with the development of an information processing system capable of handling these needs. In addition to planning and implementation, the coordinator will be expected to train and assist users of these systems to ensure that district employees can capably carry out the many tasks necessary to manage the business functions of the organization.

To be successful in any of these major roles, it's important the technology coordinator be skilled in budgeting and planning. Since the tech coordinator typically has primary responsibility for developing and supervising the school's or district's technology plan and working with other district staff and administration to promote a shared vision for the use of technology, the coordinator must gain budgetary support for that vision and evaluate the success of the plan over time. The technology coordinator is usually expected to help find supplemental resources, such as grants and E-rate funding. By helping to establish and implement an effective technology plan—working with executive administration and the board of education to ensure the necessary budgetary support for the plan and securing supplemental funding for technology initiatives whenever possible—the technology coordinator can help ensure the most effective implementation of technology resources for teaching, learning, and business functions.

Boxed items with additional information include:

Helpful Hints. These useful ideas will help the technology coordinator deal with difficult problems and tricky situations likely faced on the job.

Toolbox Tips. Toolbox Tips are concrete recommendations for dealing with specific issues or situations. These techniques are currently used by technology coordinators in the field or are derived from resources in the literature.

Useful forms and sample policies can be found throughout the book. These appear in italic type in the table of contents.

A glossary of key terms has been included in appendix A. Glossary terms appear in *bold italic type* when first used in the text. Appendix B provides sample job descriptions, appendix C is a mini-grant application form and budget, appendix D contains a bibliography, and the National Educational Technology Standards for Administrators (NETS·A) can be found in appendix E.

A Guide and a Reference

We hope this handbook will serve as a useful guide and reference. We've attempted to structure the handbook so that it can be used in a variety of different ways: as a guide for understanding essential questions, as a reference for finding useful information, and as a model for identifying the wide variety of tasks and responsibilities faced by technology coordinators.

This handbook can be read from beginning to end, but it can also be used as a reference tool and accessed as needed to find information on a particular area of interest. Skimming the entire handbook should provide an overview of the issues and responsibilities that make up the technology coordinator position. An in-depth reading of a single chapter should provide sufficient background on a particular area of responsibility, such as desktop support.

The handbook should also be useful in helping district administrators and board of education members understand the wide range of technology issues and questions that must be addressed to successfully use technology and integrate it into the educational process and other school district operations. Those who don't provide technological support and leadership on a daily basis may lack the in-depth understanding of the technology coordinator. The figures, examples, references, and resources of this handbook should be useful in helping them understand and address the complex issues of technology implementation.

We also hope this handbook will focus the discussion, nationwide, regarding certification standards for the technology coordinator. While we do not view this handbook as being comprehensive in addressing all issues faced by technology coordinators, we believe it's an important first step that provides both a useful model of the work performed by the technology coordinator and a functional reference for those who aspire to, or currently serve in, this important technological leadership position. We hope this handbook can serve as a beginning point in the discussion of what the important issues are and how they should be addressed to provide effective technological leadership for a school organization.

district organization

Essential Questions

1 What are the major responsibilities the technology coordinator will be expected to assume?

2 What skills and abilities will be needed to succeed in the position?

3 What day-to-day operational tasks will the technology coordinator most likely face?

4 What qualifications and job requirements are typically expected of technology coordinators?

5 What type of leadership role will the technology coordinator play in the school or district?

11

server capacity in order to support users, plan for appropriate infrastructure, and budget accordingly.

School and district administrators and office staff rely on technology to manage student information and business operations; therefore, the technology coordinator must also possess a good understanding of the *information-management* and *data-processing* needs of the organization. In a large school district, these systems may be quite complex and involve specialized programming and data processing skills that are managed by other members of the technology staff. The technology coordinator, however, must understand these systems well enough to know how to optimize the school's or district's existing technology infrastructure in order to meet those needs.

The technology coordinator's major responsibilities, then, all revolve around a single objective: to ensure that the school's or district's technology resources are being used as effectively as possible by all members of the organization—teachers, students, administrators and staff. It's important to keep this goal in mind when dealing with the widely variant, day-to-day pressures of the job.

Important decisions regarding technology should always be based on careful research and planning, and final design choices should be both manageable and feasible. Without proper information, poor decisions and

toolbox tip

"Johnny Techno-seed"

The technology coordinator will always be expected to play a variety of roles within the organization. These may include:

- The "techno janitor," who cleans up the messes and solves the problems that often occur when technology is used in the classroom.

- The "software policeman," who monitors the installation of software programs and patiently explains why the single copy of a particular program cannot be installed on all the computers in the lab.

- The technology advocate, or "Johnny Techno-seed," who plants the seeds of technology integration throughout the organization, nurtures them for a short time, and then moves on after they take root and begin to grow.

costly mistakes can be made. A major role of the technology coordinator is to gather and maintain the essential information required for good decision making. The technology coordinator must be able to determine and articulate how technology will be used organization-wide and use this information to make effective decisions and communicate them to administrators, teachers, and other district staff (Jewell, 1999).

Essential Skills and Qualifications

Certain skills are necessary in order to be successful as a technology coordinator. One of the most important is a good understanding of the role of the teacher in the educational process, preferably from actual classroom experience as a teacher. The tech coordinator needs to be able to see things from a teacher's perspective to effectively support and advocate technology integration in the classroom.

While not all schools have chosen an experienced educator as their technology coordinator, those who have selected noneducators have sometimes found limitations in what they can do (Bushweller, 1996). This position does require certain technical skills, and as *educational technology* becomes ever more complex, a technical background will become increasingly valuable. However, tech coordinators typically spend more time teaching people how to use technology than they do working with the hardware and software itself. They're often responsible, for example, for designing and implementing inservice technology instruction for teachers and staff members. This requires both the ability to communicate effectively and good interpersonal skills, since the technology coordinator will need to read the comfort level of teachers and design the instruction appropriately. Coordinators must find multiple ways to promote technology competency and help teachers take the required risks to implement technology in their classrooms (Hoffman, 1996), and those who understand what teachers go through on a day-to-day basis will likely be far more successful at it.

Teaching experience is also useful for technology coordinators because it helps them conceptualize how technology can be effectively integrated in a classroom setting to enhance learning. A coordinator who's able to demonstrate a practical understanding of classroom dynamics and basic pedagogy has a much greater chance of convincing teachers that technology integration is both desirable and doable.

Other essential qualifications for technology coordinators include strong skills in leadership, organization, and communication. Since a great deal of their work involves gathering, synthesizing, and disseminating a wealth of information about technology, coordinators must be both highly analytic and personable. On any given day, they'll need to work with a wide variety of people at many different levels, both inside and outside the organization—students, teachers, administrators, kitchen staff, board of education members, community representatives, vendors, and so forth. Technology coordinators need solid writing skills to compose effective and persuasive reports, Web pages, support e-mails, policies, and handouts. Strong telephone and speaking skills are vital, too. Experience with community relations can be very useful, since coordinators often help schools promote technology through events such as "technology night" and through presentations to the board of education and other community groups. Working with diverse groups and communicating effectively in a variety of ways are a major part of the day-to-day work of a technology coordinator.

Even though we've been emphasizing the nontechnical skills technology coordinators need to bring to their work, it's undeniable that technical qualifications are important as well. In addition to proficiency in diagnosing and solving problems with hardware and software, coordinators should be knowledgeable about trends and new developments in the field of educational technology. Although the technology coordinator may not be directly responsible for solving all technical problems, familiarity with the school's or district's technology resources and the ability to diagnose and solve general problems as they arise are essential skills.

Finally, technology coordinators need to possess planning, budgeting, and information management skills. *Technology plans* must be developed, implemented and updated on a regular basis. Budgets for the purchase and maintenance of technology resources will have to be matched to the needs of the school or district and carefully managed. Inventories of district equipment and materials must be gathered, stored, and updated on a regular basis.

Needless to say, the ideal technology coordinator would have qualifications that range from network management to teacher education to public relations. No individual is likely to possess all these skills when beginning in the position; rather, these skills will be developed over time. Probably the most useful skill will be a lifelong dedication to learning. The tech coordinator will constantly be faced with learning new things, adapting to new situations, and researching techniques and equipment on the leading edge. The ability to learn and adapt to myriad situations will serve the technology coordinator well.

SAMPLE JOB DESCRIPTION

Job descriptions for the technology coordinator position have varied widely depending on the needs of the organization and the technological savvy of administrators. Some technology coordinators have emerged from the business world with an MBA and impressive technical experience but no formal training in education (Bushweller, 1996). Many others started out as teachers and entered their positions with little formal training, minimal administrative support, and at times no real job description (Jewell, 1999).

The job description for the technology coordinator of a small rural district may be quite different from that used in a large urban or suburban district. A coordinator in a small district may be responsible for doing *all* technology-related tasks—from planning and troubleshooting to training and budgeting. In a larger organization, a professional staff may be available to maintain the network and servers and offer hardware support, allowing the tech coordinator to concentrate on staff development and the integration of technology into the curriculum. Whatever the size of the organization, however, it's important that the job description accurately describe the expectations, qualifications, and responsibilities of the position.

The following job description offers some generally accepted ideas about what schools and districts are looking for in applicants for technology coordinator positions. This generic description was compiled from a variety of job descriptions posted by districts across the nation. While these districts were diverse in their needs and requirements, common elements have been combined to identify the essential skills, requirements, and responsibilities typically expected of this position. This description can serve both as an example of how the position may be described on a job-notice board and as a model for developing a more specific description suitable to the needs of a particular organization. See appendix B for more examples.

job description

TITLE

District Technology Coordinator

JOB GOAL

Serves as the technology coordinator to plan, develop, implement, evaluate, and maintain an exemplary first-class technology program for the district. This will include support for students, teachers, support staff, and administrative staff.

QUALIFICATIONS

- Master's degree in technology, education, or related field.

- Knowledge and understanding of the field of educational technology.

- Successful experience in the use of technology in a K–12 school district.

- Demonstrated ability to work with people as part of a team.

- Leadership and organizational skills.

- Ability to effectively relate to students, teachers, and other staff.

PERFORMANCE RESPONSIBILITIES

- Provide visionary leadership and articulate that vision in areas of responsibility.

- Build working relationships with key community leaders and organizations.

- Develop plans to increase the level of technological literacy for students, faculty, and staff.

- Assist the district in developing and implementing an educational technology infrastructure that meets system-wide needs.

- Provide leadership in technology training, resources acquisition, and staff development.

- Design, coordinate, and provide educational technology inservice opportunities for school-based personnel.

- Administer and manage the district intranet for sharing information internally with staff, and develop pages and information to be placed on the public Web site.

- Assist educators in using and integrating technology in the instructional program.

- Model effective uses of appropriate instructional technology in the classroom and the school media center.

- Support teacher and student use of computers in classrooms.

- Provide staff with information about technology developments in their specific area of responsibility.

- Provide day-to-day management of such technology department personnel as network administrators, PC technicians, help-desk operators, and others who work to support technology operations.

- Develop a system-wide technology plan, evaluate it annually, and modify it as needed.

- Recommend budget requirements to effectively support the district technology plan.

- Prepare and present reports on technology issues as directed by the superintendent and board of education.

SALARY RANGE

$40,000 to $60,000 (*Authors' Note:* The salary will be dependent on experience, specific responsibilities, and the size of the district. The most common range should be $40,000 to $60,000. For a very large district, the salary range may be as high as $70,000 to $90,000.)

The Technology Coordinator Issues Model

In most schools and districts, the technology coordinator serves in a leadership position within the organizational structure. However, tech coordinators are often hired and work under the union-negotiated agreement as a teacher leader rather than as a district administrator; in other words, though they have a title and hold a position of responsibility, they may not actually be an administrator. Many districts have preferred to keep the technology coordinator as part of the teaching staff, even though the coordinator may have supervisory responsibilities and work with adults rather than children. The actual job title varies considerably from district to district—from "coordinator" to "director" to "specialist." Regardless of the title, though, the responsibilities and issues that people in this position typically face are usually quite similar.

The technology coordinator is the person who blazes a trail for technology in the school or district and understands how all the hardware, software, policies, and procedures fit together in the big picture of the school's or district's technology implementation (Jewell, 1999). The tech coordinator should be prepared to help teachers, staff, administrators, and board of education members use technology more effectively and meet the standards and goals laid out in the district's technology plan. The coordinator must find and accumulate adequate funding and administrative support to make the school's or district's technology initiatives feasible, as well as budget successfully for the necessary resources for installation, maintenance, and training (Ritchie, 1996).

The Technology Coordinator Issues Model in Figure 2 is intended to provide a complete overview of the various areas of responsibility that comprise the technology coordinator position. The model articulates several specific issues within each general area that most technology coordinators will have to address to effectively support and integrate technology use in all aspects of the organization.

Technology Coordinator Issues Model—Areas and Issues

BUDGETING AND PLANNING

- Technology Planning
- Budgeting
- Evaluation
- Grants
- E-rate Applications

TEACHING AND LEARNING

- Educational Software
- Curriculum Integration
- Instructional Technology Research
- Staff Development
- Web-Based Resources and Instruction

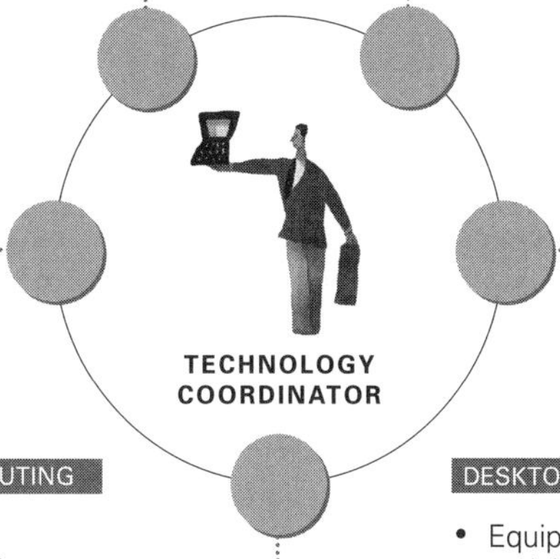

TECHNOLOGY COORDINATOR

ADMINISTRATIVE COMPUTING

- Processing Grades and Student Records
- Human Resources
- Business Operations
- Document Imaging and Management

DESKTOP SUPPORT

- Equipment Purchasing and Allocation
- Ergonomics and Furniture
- Software Licensing
- Help-Desk Support
- Equipment Repairs
- Virus Protection
- Maintenance and Upgrades

NETWORK OPERATIONS

- Network Infrastructure
- User Management
- E-Mail System Management
- Backup Procedures
- Remote Management
- Intranet Management

FIGURE 2

Real-Life Technology Coordinators

The following profiles depict the varying work environments and job descriptions typical of the technology coordinator position in small, medium, and large school districts around the country.

Meet Susan R., Technology Coordinator for a Rural District

Susan R. works as the technology coordinator for a rural Midwest school district. She's the only technology staff member for the district, which serves an agricultural town of about 10,000 people. The district has five school buildings, with a total enrollment of 1,200 students in Grades K–12.

Susan serves the district as network administrator, performs hardware maintenance and repair, handles the purchasing and installation of equipment and software, manages the technology inventory, develops short- and long-range technology goals, and manages all technology spending. She provides professional development in technology for all employees of the school system. Her responsibilities also include directing the technology committee responsible for developing and carrying out the technology plan and for implementing technology integration activities in district classrooms.

Thanks to her considerable experience in working with schools and teachers, Susan has been successful in implementing special technology initiatives in her district. She was instrumental in initiating a plan providing seventh-graders with handheld computers—a program that's been successful with both teachers and students. One of the secrets to her success has been the development of a cadre of district teachers and administrators who assist her with planning, decision making, staff training, and implementation activities. Susan is also active in technology leadership activities in her state. She has twice served as the president of the statewide computers-in-education organization.

Susan came to this position from outside education and has never worked as a teacher. She received her computer training through a vocational program and does not have a four-year college degree. She's been working in this position for nine years and works on an 11-month-contract basis. Her salary range for this position is $35,000–$45,000.

Meet Sam T., Technology Coordinator for a Small Urban District

Sam T. is the general director of information services for a Midwest school district in a state capital with a population of 130,000. The district serves 14,000 students in Grades K–12, with 37 instructional sites and additional support sites, service centers, and office locations.

Sam deals with management and administration of all aspects of information and communication technology for the district, including voice, video, and data services. His duties include development of the district technology plan, implementation of several technology-themed magnet schools, and planning and development of a high-speed network capable of carrying data, voice, and video to all schools. His office is responsible for budgeting, purchasing, installation, and support of all district technologies. His staff of 20 includes PC and network technicians, network administrators, help-desk operators, professional development trainers, instructional specialists, programmers, computer operators, and technicians.

Sam began his work with information technology while serving in the Navy for 10 years. After leaving the military, he earned a bachelor's degree in education and worked as a secondary math teacher for several years. Later, Sam worked in the business field and gained experience in developing, implementing, and using information technology services in business.

Sam spent 12 years working for the district in various aspects of information technology before coming into his current position four years ago. He's earning additional college credit in educational administration coursework.

Sam and his 15-member technology team work on a 12-month-contract basis. The salary range for his position is $70,000–$80,000.

Meet Ted B., Technology Coordinator for a Large Urban District

For three years, Ted B. has been the director of instructional technology for a diverse, urban school district in a Midwestern state's largest city. More than 100 instructional sites are located across this city of 400,000, serving more than 48,000 students in a wide variety of traditional schools, magnet schools, and special programs.

Ted has worked in education for 22 years as a classroom teacher, building administrator, and district administrator. He also worked at the state's department of education. Originally trained as an elementary teacher, he earned a master's degree in educational administration and has been working with different aspects of technology for the last eight years.

As a mid-level administrator for a large district, Ted supervises a staff of eight instructional technology specialists who promote and implement the instructional use of technology. They provide professional development in instructional programs, support special education projects using technology, and provide schools, teachers, and classrooms with support for using technology in a learning environment. Ted and his staff are also responsible for developing the district-level technology plan in collaboration with other departments and for writing grant applications for special projects that offer unique opportunities to use technology.

As part of a large urban district, Ted has the freedom to concentrate on the instructional aspects of technology. Other departments within the district handle hardware and software support, network services, purchasing and installation of computer equipment, and administrative computing functions, such as data processing.

Working in a large bureaucracy has both advantages and disadvantages. Ted and his staff are free to concentrate on strictly instructional issues, but often their work is dependent on the work of other departments. Developing positive relationships with these departments through frequent and effective communication has been essential.

Ted and his staff work on a 12-month-contract basis. The salary range for his position is $80,000–$90,000.

ANSWERS TO
Essential Questions

1 What are the major responsibilities the technology coordinator will be expected to assume?

The technology coordinator is expected to help establish the vision for technology in the school or district, create policies which support that vision, train staff to make progress toward the vision, and assist end users to solve problems associated with technology.

2 What skills and abilities will be needed to succeed in the position?

To be successful in this position, the technology coordinator will need a combination of strong interpersonal skills, effective problem-solving skills, leadership and planning skills, and technical skills.

3 What day-to-day operational tasks will the technology coordinator most likely face?

The technology coordinator will be expected to conduct staff development training sessions, work with users to solve problems and answer questions, communicate with vendors, meet with district administrators to plan or develop policy, and speak to community groups about district technology initiatives. The technology coordinator is often responsible for the management of other technology personnel, such as network administrators, computer technicians, help-desk operators, and building-level technology specialists. The development and update of the district Web site and the administration of the district intranet are also regular duties that fall in the domain of the technology coordinator.

4 What qualifications and job requirements are typically expected of technology coordinators?

As part of their position, technology coordinators are expected to provide leadership, build relationships, offer assistance, model effective usage, assist teachers and students, plan and evaluate hardware and software purchases, administer maintenance programs, and make budgetary decisions.

5 What type of leadership role will the technology coordinator play in the school or district?

The technology coordinator will be expected to assist the administration and the board of education in establishing the school or district technology plan. The coordinator is expected to ensure the success of all school or district technology initiatives—from budgeting to purchasing to training to troubleshooting—in order to make the district technology vision a reality.

Resources

PRINT RESOURCES

Baylor, A. L., & Ritchie, D. (2002). What factors facilitate teacher skill, teacher morale, and perceived student learning in technology-using classrooms? *Computers and Education, 39*(4), 395-414.

Bushweller, K. (1996). How mighty is your wizard? *The American School Board Journal, 183*(5), a14-a16.

Durost, R. A. (1994). Integrating computer technology: Planning, training, and support. *NASSP Bulletin, 78*(1), 49-54.

Grohe, B., & Levinson, E. (2002). Managing technology is different. *Converge, 5*(1), 42-43.

Hoffman, B. (1996). Managing the information revolution: Planning the integration of school technology. *NASSP Bulletin, 80*(2), 89-98.

Holland, L., & Moore-Steward, T. (2000). A different divide: Preparing tech savvy leaders. *Leadership, 30*(1), 6-10.

Jewell, M. (1999). The art and craft of technology leadership. *Learning and Leading with Technology, 26*(4), 46-47.

Maddux, C. (2002). Information technology in education: The critical lack of principled leadership. *Educational Technology, 42*(3), 41-50.

Marcovitz, D. M. (1998). *Supporting technology in schools: The roles of computer coordinators*. Washington, DC: Society for Information Technology and Teacher Education Conference Proceedings. (ERIC Document Reproduction Service No. ED421150)

Moursund, D. (1992). *The technology coordinator*. Eugene, OR: International Society for Technology in Education.

Ritchie, D. (1996). The administrative role in the integration of technology. *NASSP Bulletin, 80*(2), 42-51.

ONLINE RESOURCES

Redefining the Role of the Technology Coordinator: **www.cahe.nmsu.edu/ bchamberlin/techcoord/welcome.html**

School-Based Technology Coordinator's Home Page: **www.schools.pinellas.k12.fl.us/tchandbk/default.htm**

School District Technology Coordinator: **http://arkedu.state.ar.us/ade-guide/ tech_coord.html**

Technology Coordinator Resources: **http://home.socal.rr.com/exworthy/tc.htm**

The Technology Coordinator's Web Site: **www.ac.wwu.edu/~kenr/TCsite/contents.html**

Technology Leaders Resource Center: **www.minot.com/~nansen/**

teaching and learning

Essential Questions

1 How can the technology coordinator assist with the selection and purchase of effective educational and desktop software?

2 How can the technology coordinator help teachers integrate technology into the curriculum?

3 What instructional technology research should the technology coordinator do to investigate the effectiveness of technology use in classrooms?

4 How can the technology coordinator plan and implement an effective staff development program?

5 How can the technology coordinator use Web-based resources to support teachers and students?

The work of the technology coordinator is important to all areas of the educational organization, but most crucially so in the areas of teaching and learning. By inspiring teachers to use technology effectively in the classroom, it's in these two areas that tech coordinators can have the greatest impact on student education and motivation (Figure 3).

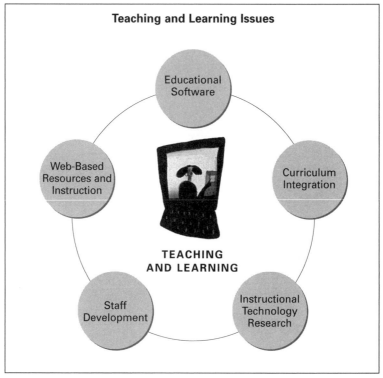

Teaching and Learning Issues

Educational Software

Web-Based Resources and Instruction

Curriculum Integration

TEACHING AND LEARNING

Staff Development

Instructional Technology Research

FIGURE 3

Selecting Educational Software

The careful selection of educational software is very important to the success of a school's or district's technology integration efforts. The technology coordinator must first determine which software will serve as the standard installation on each computer in the organization. This set of software comprises the basic set of tools available to all users.

While districts may prefer one manufacturer over another, each computer should be outfitted with a minimum set of standard software: a word processing program for writing and editing text, a spreadsheet program for working with numbers, a database program for organizing and manipulating data, a desktop publishing program for creating publications of various types, a presentation program for creating and organizing multimedia presentations, an e-mail client for communicating, and a browser program for accessing information on the Internet.

This core software should become the basis for all machine setups and serve as the basic kit for the integration of technology into teaching and learning (McGillivray, 1999). Any users who access the technology resources within the organization can be sure they will find these standard tools installed and available for use. McGillivray points out that "because the tools are used across the curriculum, students learn to use them in multiple venues. Each teacher contributes to the student's mastery of the tools. Because the students use the tools frequently, their mastery becomes more rapid and their work more sophisticated" (p. 46).

Figure 4 illustrates the software kit implemented by the Heidelberg Model Schools. This kit contains a set of common software programs that are installed and used to support the integration of technology into all classrooms and subject areas. By selecting common tools for communications, word processing, presentations, computation, reference, security, and administration, the school was able to minimize costs, provide universal access, and address a wide range of classroom activities and projects. The selection of common tools for all classrooms also minimized the support requirements by making the number of programs more manageable (McGillivray).

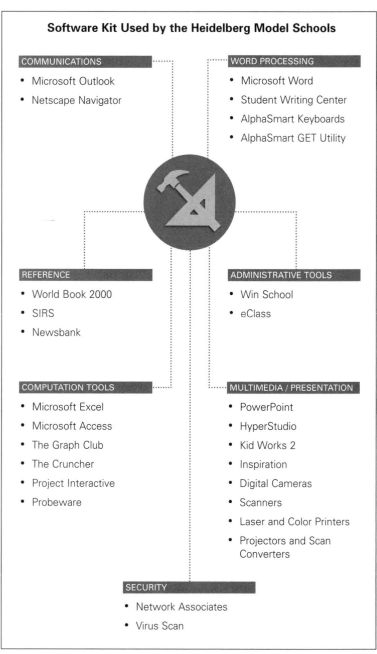

Software Kit Used by the Heidelberg Model Schools

COMMUNICATIONS
- Microsoft Outlook
- Netscape Navigator

WORD PROCESSING
- Microsoft Word
- Student Writing Center
- AlphaSmart Keyboards
- AlphaSmart GET Utility

REFERENCE
- World Book 2000
- SIRS
- Newsbank

ADMINISTRATIVE TOOLS
- Win School
- eClass

COMPUTATION TOOLS
- Microsoft Excel
- Microsoft Access
- The Graph Club
- The Cruncher
- Project Interactive
- Probeware

MULTIMEDIA / PRESENTATION
- PowerPoint
- HyperStudio
- Kid Works 2
- Inspiration
- Digital Cameras
- Scanners
- Laser and Color Printers
- Projectors and Scan Converters

SECURITY
- Network Associates
- Virus Scan

FIGURE 4

The programs included in the Heidelberg Model Schools software kit included some of the most common programs installed on desktop computers in schools today. They're by no means the only choices a district can make in adopting a standard set of software tools for use by teachers, students, and staff. In addition to commercial programs such as these, a wide variety of freeware and shareware products are available from many developers and sources found on the Internet.

Often, these freeware and shareware products may lack the name recognition of more commonly known and used products, such as those shown in Figure 4, but they may offer similar functionality for a fraction of the cost. The StarOffice suite of programs offers the same functionality as the more commonly known products from Microsoft and is essentially free to educational institutions. More information on this suite of programs can be found at **www.sun.com/software/star/staroffice/**. These programs are also designed to share files and be interoperable with Microsoft programs.

Alternatives to Microsoft products also exist for e-mail services for both servers and desktop computers. Pegasus mail offers the Mercury Mail Transport System for servers, as well as the Pegasus Mail client for desktops, as a free download from the Pegasus site (**www.pmail.com**). The software is free, but users do have to pay for user manuals and support. These fees, however, are minimal, even for a large organization.

The technology coordinator will also play an integral role in the selection of additional software for use in the classroom. Information about specific programs and vendors must be gathered, software reviews located and distributed, and comparisons made of the programs' various capabilities and how they might support the school's or district's goals for technology use and integration.

It's important that the tech coordinator solicit input from staff and teachers before making final software selections. These users will have a better understanding of the curriculum and how the software can support it and will ultimately be the ones to use the software to support learning. Allowing end users a strong voice in purchasing decisions will lead to greater support and, ultimately, more frequent use of the software. The coordinator can effectively guide this process by acting as the liaison who contacts vendors, conducts research on new programs, tests the software on district computers, contacts other schools or districts to see what products they're using, and reports to the school software committees that will make the final selections.

The technology coordinator also plays a vital role in obtaining the best price for such purchases by engaging in the *bid request* process, working with consortia to make bulk purchases and working with vendors to secure the best pricing available. Throughout the selection process, the technology coordinator should work to ensure that the software packages chosen match the educational goals and long-range technology plans for the school or district.

helpful hint

Online Database

It's important to make sure that software evaluation information is available to staff members searching for educational software. One way to do this is the creation of an online database of software evaluation information that can be easily accessed, reviewed, and added to as products are reviewed. Database programs such as Filemaker Pro (www.filemaker.com) make it easy to share information over a network or the Web by publishing databases on a Web site. The program comes with 30 starter solutions that can be adapted to the user's particular needs. Creating and posting such a database will help staff members more easily find useful software and avoid wasting time with inferior products someone has already tried and reviewed.

One way that technology coordinators can demonstrate their leadership and improve this process is to implement standard procedures for the selection of classroom software. Many valuable education dollars have been misspent on software programs that did not work as intended, were not compatible with or appropriate for the school's or district's hardware, or did not address an appropriate district educational need. An effective way to guard against this is to implement standard forms, criteria, and selection procedures for the purchase of educational software.

The first step should be to establish a software adoption committee. This committee—made up of representatives from different grade levels and subject areas—is charged with the evaluation of purchasing requests for educational software programs. This committee should meet as needed to review software recommendations and work with the technology coordinator to make final purchasing decisions.

Standard software review forms should be developed and used to gather information about products that staff members wish to purchase. These forms should require individuals requesting the purchase to gather basic product information, specify how the software would be used educationally as well as what content and technology standards it would address, list specific hardware requirements, summarize relevant software review articles, and submit all of this information to the software selection committee. The software selection committee would then evaluate the information and recommendations submitted to them by staff members, make selections based on those recommendations, and work with the technology coordinator to make final purchasing and budget decisions.

toolbox tip

Software Form

Software selection is an important yet time-consuming task that can benefit considerably from well-defined procedures. Making use of a software selection form such as the following can help standardize the process and make selection decisions more informed and effective. This form should identify useful information about the product and how it will be used in an educational setting. This information can be quite helpful when making software purchasing decisions.

software selection form

Name

School

Grade or Department

Software Title

Publisher

Content Area

Topic

Targeted Grade Level

TYPE OF LICENSE TO BE PURCHASED *(CHECK ONE)*

☐ Single Computer   ☐ Site License

☐ Lab Pack   ☐ Network License

TECHNICAL REQUIREMENTS

	Computer / Processor Required		Hard-Drive Space Required
	RAM Required		Additional Hardware Required
	Compatibility With Existing Software		Other Requirements

SOFTWARE CATEGORY

☐ Presentation   ☐ Multimedia

☐ Simulation   ☐ Data Processing

☐ Tutorial   ☐ Educational Game

☐ Reference   ☐ Graphics

software selection form

☐ Authoring   ☐ Word Processing

☐ Drill and Practice   ☐ Handheld Application

☐ Other (please specify)

SOFTWARE FEATURES

Claim	Strongly Agree	Agree	Disagree	N/A
The directions are clear and easy to follow.				
It's easy to start and exit the program.				
Users can easily resume where they left off in the program.				
The program functions well and is free of bugs.				
The program is enjoyable to use.				
The graphic elements are meaningful and appropriate.				
Sound can be turned on and off.				
The software contains useful management features.				
Basic tasks are easily learned and intuitive.				
Advanced features are easy to access and apply.				
Menu-driven tutorials are built into the program.				

software selection form

What specific curricular and technology standards will be addressed by this software?

_____

_____

What are your instructional goals for using this software?

_____

_____

Have you found reviews of this software? If so, summarize comments from the reviews:

_____

_____

Have you tested the software in the classroom? If so, summarize what you did with the software, and rate its usefulness to the learning process:

_____

_____

If you haven't used the software before, do you know colleagues who have? If so, indicate how they used the software and their general evaluation:

_____

_____

Other comments or information:

_____

_____

software selection form

Page 4

PURCHASING INFORMATION

Cost _____

Product ID Number _____

Recommended Vendor _____

Vendor Address _____

Vendor Phone Number _____

Software Selection
Committee Comments _____

_____

_____

Committee Purchase
Recommendation ☐ Yes ☐ No

Technology Coordinator Notes

Date of purchase _____

Software license number _____

Installation information,
notes,and location(s) _____

_____

_____

Integrating Technology Into the Curriculum

The technology coordinator will spend considerable time working with teachers to help them integrate technology into new or existing curriculum. It's easy for teachers to fall into the trap of assuming that the way they've been doing things for years is fully acceptable, even optimal; it's difficult, sometimes, to dissuade them from this and encourage them to try new things. As Wasser (1996) aptly points out, "Learning to function effectively in technologically rich environments is a complex developmental process for individuals and the systems in which they work" (p. 1). To change the way they teach and the materials they use requires time, commitment, risk taking, adequate resources, and consistent and patient support. The technology coordinator needs to be able to inspire teachers with a vision of how effective technology integration can benefit them and demonstrate activities, lesson plans, and processes that make exciting use of technology resources.

One way to start is by offering a variety of informal professional development opportunities where teachers can learn more about the technology resources that are available to them for use in the classroom. By offering a variety of courses in an informal, collegial setting, the technology coordinator can familiarize teachers with new hardware and software resources without intimidating them. The coordinator can also listen to teachers' concerns and questions and clear up misconceptions.

Once teachers become comfortable using technology for their own purposes, they'll find it easier to devise ways to implement the same technology in their classrooms. Regularly scheduled technology sessions can be offered before or after school, during the lunch hour or planning time, or on a release-time basis. These sessions can be set up to teach a particular skill or introduce a new idea, but more important, they should establish a venue for teachers to experiment and become comfortable with technology.

Study groups can also be an effective way for teachers to study a new technology in depth and learn from one another as they develop their skills. Whatever method you choose, this training is critical to the successful integration of technology within the organization: "A one-size-fits-all professional development approach generally does not work in the face of the great diversity of technology readiness and ability" (Wasser, 1996, p. 3).

To ensure teachers are provided with the training and resources they need, it's important for the technology coordinator to confirm that a standard set of technology resources is available in all classrooms, and that additional, specialized technology tools are available in libraries and media centers. A classroom should be outfitted with at least one multimedia desktop computer and such standard software as word processing, spreadsheet, database, and desktop publishing programs, as well as an e-mail client and Internet browser. Libraries or computer labs should be furnished with additional equipment such as digital cameras, scanners, image-editing software, storage devices, CD and *DVD* burners, and digital video-editing equipment. Providing a variety of resources in various locations around the school helps ensure that teachers and students have ready access to the resources they need to carry out myriad learning activities.

toolbox tip

Mini-Grants

Mini-grants are a great opportunity to promote technology integration and provide incentive for staff to find new ways to use technology in their work. Offering larger grants for cooperative projects helps get more than one teacher involved. Teachers who have completed a mini-grant project should be required to offer a staff development session so that other staff members can learn from their experiences.

A mini-grant program could be funded in a variety of ways. Professional development funds from either the technology budget or the general professional development budget could be used to fund such a program. Grant funds from federal, state, or private sources could be used to support a mini-grant program if the grant were written to include the support. Another source of funding would be the Title II–Part D funds for improving teacher quality through the use of technology. An example of a mini-grant application form can be found in appendix C.

To enhance the use of technology in classrooms, it's often beneficial to organize and administer a mini-grant program that provides special funding for new and innovative projects. Mini-grant programs can provide

The guide offers a variety of helpful suggestions and ideas, including a flowchart of the evaluation process, examples of formative and summative evaluation questions, tips on where to begin, data that should be collected, questions to ask, and forms and worksheets to use in the process. The guide also contains a variety of sample surveys that can be used as is or adapted to meet the particular needs of the evaluation project.

Technology in Schools: Suggestions, Tools and Guidelines for Assessing Technology in Elementary and Secondary Education is a more recent publication funded by the National Center for Educational Statistics. It was developed to help decision makers who are interested in technology to prepare, collect, and assess information about if and how technology is being used in their school systems. It's organized around important key questions, and the principles are grouped into seven primary topics. These topics include technology planning and policies, finance, equipment and infrastructure, technology applications (software and systems), maintenance and support, professional development, and technology integration. For each of these topics, key questions are identified and guidance given on how best these questions can be answered through the collection of data and records.

While this document is quite useful in identifying both the questions and the information necessary to answer the questions, ultimately it's up to those conducting the evaluation to determine if their needs and goals are being met.

Planning and Implementing a Staff Development Program

One of the most challenging and important tasks a technology coordinator will face is the creation of a staff development program for all employees of the school or district. Effective staff development was one of the four pillars described in 1996 by President Bill Clinton when he articulated a vision for technology use in schools through the Technology Literacy Challenge Fund. The four pillars of this initiative are:

1 Provide all teachers the training and support they need to help students learn through computers and the information super-highway;

2 Develop effective and engaging software and online learning resources as an integral part of the school curriculum;

3 Provide access to modern computers for all teachers and students;

4 Connect every school and classroom in America to the information superhighway.

A successful staff development program will allow a school district to prepare teachers (and, in turn, students) to use technology as a natural part of the curriculum.

Often a district begins by teaching "tool"-related courses to teachers and staff. These courses help people more effectively use their computers and installed software programs. These types of courses do not do much, however, to help teachers learn how to integrate technology into their instructional practices. Effective staff development programs will focus on the larger goal of improved student learning and performance, rather than on learning technology as a goal in and of itself: "Learning to use Microsoft Word is not the same process as learning to teach writing across the curriculum using Word" (Peterman, McGillivray, & Frantz, 1998, Hanau American Schools section, para. 13).

The technology coordinator must work with teachers and the school or district administration to determine staff development needs and design a program to meet those needs. A good place to begin is with a review of the district or building technology plan. The technology plan is the guiding document that lays out the road map of where the organization wants to go with technology and how it plans to get there. To develop an effective technology staff development program, the program must be tied to the goals and intentions of the larger plan for technology in the district. Reviewing the district technology plan will help the technology coordinator and other stakeholders clearly understand what sorts of skills and dispositions are important and what work needs to be done to design a program that will develop them.

It's also important for those planning a technology staff development program to look at the national standards for students, teachers, and administrators. The International Society for Technology in Education developed these standards in conjunction with a variety of educational leadership organizations, curriculum organizations, the U.S. Department of Education, NASA, and several private organizations. More information about these standards, along with a variety of supporting resources, can be found at **http://cnets.iste.org**. These standards provide guidance on what skills should be learned, when they should be taught, and how technology can be used to support new learning environments. They have been adopted by a number of states and serve as the basis for the standards used in other states. The standards and related resources provide a solid basis for determining what teachers and administrators should learn as part of a technology staff development program.

No staff development program will be successful without acknowledging what skills people already have and what they already know. It's important for the technology coordinator to have an understanding of the thoughts and desires of the people taking part in the staff development program. By conducting a series of focus group conversations with teachers and staff members representative of various departments, grade levels, and schools from across the district, it will be possible for the tech coordinator to have a clear understanding of the staff's professional development needs.

In addition to focus groups to gather data on the current technology skill level and needs of district staff, it's useful to use surveys and other assessment tools. A variety of online tools and resources exist for conducting such surveys and assessments. Dr. Chris Moersch has developed a helpful assessment tool with his Levels of Technology Integration surveys, which can be found online at **www.peak.org/~labquest/NBEA/**. Another useful tool for self-assessment of staff technology skills is the Profiler online collaboration tool from the High Plains Regional Technology in Education Consortium (HPR*TEC) found online at **http://profiler.hprtec.org**. This free tool allows users to take surveys online to assess technology skills and abilities. Technology coordinators can also register as district administrators so that they can develop and modify surveys of their own and download data results from the site. The site also includes access to surveys based on the ISTE standards.

Once the technology coordinator has gathered all the pertinent information from surveys and assessments, an effective program can be planned and implemented. The program should include a variety of learning opportunities and interventions that are available in a number of different formats. Teachers may learn by taking classes, working individually with the technology coordinator to develop and teach lessons, participating in a study group, attending a conference, or collaborating with other staff members on a technology project, or all of the above. Without this training and support, teachers are likely to use the technology resources available to them only for lower-level tasks, such as word processing. Those who have received the necessary assistance and training, on the other hand, will tend to use technology for higher-level activities such as data collection and analysis, complex problem solving, and Internet research. Effective professional development will support teachers' efforts to integrate technology broadly and deeply into their professional practice and school life (Wasser & McNamara, 1998).

Incorporating Web-Based Resources and Instruction

The Internet offers the technology coordinator marvelous resources for use in the coordinator's own job position, and it's also a wonderful source for instructional materials: "The Internet, more so than any technology that has preceded it, provides students with access to a vast array of information and resources far greater than could ever be provided within the four walls of a classroom" (U.S. Department of Education, 2000a, p. 31). The tech coordinator should be adept at finding and organizing the wide array of resources and materials that exist on the Internet in order to inform classroom teachers about them.

The technology coordinator should also find ways to share and publicize some of the many sites and resources available to enhance instruction. One way to do this is to create a links section for the district Web site. This site can be updated regularly and can contain organized and categorized links to resources on the Internet. Another method for sharing information of this type is through a regular publication, either print or electronic, that

Resources

PRINT RESOURCES

McGillivray, K. (1999). The tool kit: An innovative approach to technology integration in networked schools. *Learning and Leading with Technology, 26*(5), 45-49.

Wasser, J., & McNamara, E. (1998). Professional development and full school technology integration. *Hanau Model Schools Partnership Research Brief #5.* Cambridge, MA: TERC.

ONLINE RESOURCES

Byrom, E. (2001). *Factors influencing the effective use of technology for teaching and learning.* Retrieved December 12, 2001, from **www.seirtec.org/publications/lessons.pdf**

CEO Forum on Education and Technology. (1997). *From pillars to progress.* Retrieved March 26, 2000, from **www.ceoforum.org/reports.cfm?RID=1**

CEO Forum School Technology and Readiness Chart: **www.ceoforum.org/starchart.cfm**

An Educator's Guide to Evaluating the Use of Technology in Schools and Classrooms: **www.ed.gov/pubs/EdTechGuide/index.html**

enGauge Online Framework for Assessment and Planning: **www.ncrel.org/engauge/**

Heidelberg Model Schools Partnership: **www.hmsp.org**

High Plains Regional Technology Consortium: **www.hprtec.org**

International Society for Technology in Education: **www.iste.org**

Mid-Continent Research for Education and Learning—Technology Integration Resources: **www.mcrel.org/products/tech/technology/index.asp**

National Business Education Alliance (LoTI survey): **www.peak.org/~labquest/NBEA/**

National Educational Technology Standards Project: **http://cnets.iste.org**

National Staff Development Council: **www.nsdc.org**

Peterman, L., McGillivray, K., & Frantz, J. (1998). Professional development: From reports to reality. *LNT Perspectives*. Retrieved November 11, 2001, from **www.edc.org/LNT/news/Issue6/feature.htm**

Profiler Online Collaboration and Assessment Tool: **http://profiler.hprtec.org**

Technology Applications Center for Educator Development—Assessment Tools: **www.tcet.unt.edu/START/assess/tools.htm**

Technology in Schools. Suggestions, Tools and Guidelines for Assessing Technology in Elementary and Secondary Education: **http://nces.ed.gov/pubsearch/pubsinfo.asp?pubid=2003313**

U.S. Department of Education. (2000). *e-Learning: Putting a world class education at the fingertips of all children.* Retrieved November 22, 2001, from **www.ed.gov/Technology/elearning/e-learning.pdf**

Wasser, J. (1996). Navigating past the technology on-ramp. *Hands-On!, 19*(2). Retrieved November 11, 2001, from **www.terc.edu/handson/f96/navigating.html**

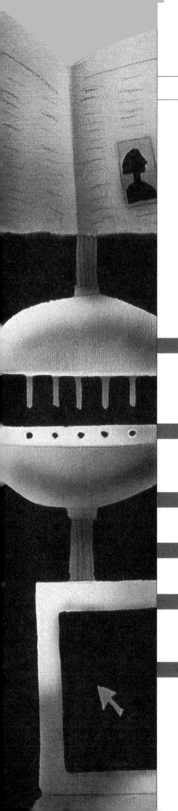

desktop support

Essential Questions

1 How can the technology coordinator assure that the purchasing, allocation, and inventory of equipment is carried out in an effective manner?

2 What must the technology coordinator know about *ergonomics* and the selection of furniture for offices and classrooms?

3 What must the technology coordinator do to ensure proper licensing of software?

4 How can the technology coordinator optimize help-desk support for end users?

5 How can the technology coordinator effectively protect computers from *viruses, worms,* and other security threats?

6 What must the technology coordinator do to make sure equipment is properly maintained, upgraded, and repaired as necessary?

Equipment Purchasing and Allocation

Part of using technology successfully is selecting the most appropriate equipment for a given situation. Equipment that doesn't meet the needs of the end user can lead to frustration and disuse. Technology coordinators are usually responsible for planning and purchasing the technology used throughout the school or district and therefore must have a solid understanding of how equipment will be used in order to make appropriate purchases and assignments. A computer appropriate for use in a fourth-grade classroom may not be the correct machine for a computer-assisted drawing lab or an office secretary. Learning how to allocate the school's or district's technology resources most effectively and equitably is a crucial part of the technology coordinator's role in desktop support.

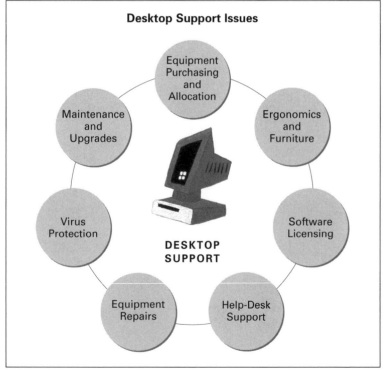

Desktop Support Issues

FIGURE 5

The technology coordinator should work with end users to develop the specifications for equipment to be purchased. It may be helpful to have different sets of specifications for particular settings: one for a standard classroom computer, for example; one for a specialized computer lab; one for an office computer; and so forth. The settings computers are used in will determine the software needed, the amount of memory required, how much access to network resources is necessary, the size of monitors that will be suitable, and the proper number of inputs for plugging in peripherals. Each of these computers may be based on a particular model from a manufacturer, but different options may be selected depending on the needs of the user and the distinctive way in which the machine will be used.

After general specifications have been developed in consultation with end users, the technology coordinator should obtain current pricing from a variety of retailers or manufacturers. Prices should then be compared. This price comparison is usually done through a competitive bid process.

A formal bid request describes the specifications of the item to be purchased, provides a timeline for when the bid must be returned, and sets a time and date for a formal bid opening. It's essential to accurately spell out all requirements in the bid request, including machine features, requirements for parts, length of warranty, and technical support issues. Failure to address an issue may lead to problems and frustrations after the purchase is complete.

The following pages show a form requesting sealed bids for the purchase of 15 projectors.

helpful hint

Government Contracts

State governments often negotiate long-term purchasing contracts with vendors who sell computers and related equipment. These contracts enable individual schools and districts to make purchases at significant savings. Technology coordinators should be able to identify vendors who are part of the state's contracted purchasing program by contacting vendors prior to purchase.

A school district's business office should have information about specific state purchasing requirements. Additional information about government contract purchasing procedures and regulations can usually be obtained by contacting the state department of education or department of administration.

request for bid

UNIFIED SCHOOL DISTRICT

123 Elm Street

Anywhere, OR 97409

Date   *May 24, 2004*

Bid No.   *0304–C–10*

To   *Jane Smith*

Sealed bids addressed to USD Purchasing Department will be received at (mailing address) until **2:00 p.m. PST on June 15, 2004,** at which time the bids will be opened and read aloud. Bid envelope shall be plainly marked:

SEALED BID FOR PROJECTORS

DO NOT OPEN BEFORE

DATE: JUNE 15, 2004, 2:00 P.M. PST

Any bid received later than the specified time, whether delivered in person or mailed, shall be disqualified. The district reserves the right to reject any or all bids, to accept the bid deemed most advantageous to the school district, and to waive any formalities of bidding.

All bidders whose domicile is located outside the state should furnish the school district with a copy of their state's preferential bidding statutes and the applicable percent received by in-state bidders from the state in which the contractor is located.

John Brown

(Purchasing/Property Manager)

School District #383

BID NO. 0304–C–10 *PROJECTORS*

DUE: JUNE 15, 2004, 2:00 P.M. PST

BID SPECIFICATIONS

This bid is for 15 projectors with the following specifications.

Technical specifications for computer projectors

Screen brightness	*Minimum 2,000 ANSI lumens*
Contrast ratio	*400:1*
Projection lamp	*200 watt UHP*
Lens type	*Manual zoom and focus*
Estimated lamp life	2,000 hours
Throw distance	*4 ft. to 25 ft.*
Native resolution	*1024 x 768 (XGA)*
Display compatibility	*SXGA, XGA, SVGA, VGA*
Computer formats	*1280 x 1024, 1024 x 768, 800 x 600, 640 x 480*
Computer inputs	*Two required: one DVI and one component in/monitor out*
Video inputs	*RCA and S-Video*
Cable	*DVI to VGA cable included*
Remote projector & mouse control	*Wireless (infrared) with laser pointer*
Carrying case	*Carrying case must be included*
Weight	*7 lbs. or less*
Warranty	*Three-year / 6,000-hour projector warranty*

request for bid

BID NO. 0304–C–10 *PROJECTORS*

DUE: JUNE 15, 2004, 2:00 P.M. PST

We have read all guidelines stated in the notice to bidders and submit this quotation in accordance with stated conditions.

Authorized Signature _____

Date _____

Company Representing _____

Questions concerning this quotation may be directed to:

_____
(please print or type name)

Telephone Number (___) _____ Fax Number (___) _____

E-mail _____

Approximate delivery date _____

Bid prices good through _____

Price per projector _____

Quantity x 15

Total Bid Price _____

The budgetary situation in many states is beginning to improve after several years in which tax collections were down significantly. While the financial situation at the state level may be improving, many school districts have seen several years of flat or declining budgets. Schools may face several more years of limited funds and continue to struggle to find the money necessary to purchase needed technology. For those school districts looking for ways to reduce hardware costs or maximize the purchasing power of their budgets, a few ideas for getting the most from hardware dollars are listed below:

toolbox tip

Drive Image

When ordering a large number of pieces of equipment, it may be useful to contract with the vendor to preinstall the desired **drive image** prior to shipment. It's often possible with volume purchasing to have a machine shipped to the school or district for software installation and setup. This machine's setup then becomes the "master" image, which the manufacturer can duplicate for all subsequent computers prior to shipping. If **cloning** machines prior to shipping is not possible, loading drive images on a local server or an external hard drive and then cloning on site may be an acceptable alternative.

- Consider factory-refurbished equipment. This equipment includes items used for demonstrations, cosmetically damaged units, and factory-defective systems. All are repaired and tested by the original equipment manufacturer (OEM). These items have been recertified to meet the original equipment specifications and are often sold with a warranty. The purchase of such equipment can yield considerable savings.

- Consider equipment that is coming "off-lease" with another organization. This is the equivalent of purchasing a program, or fleet, car from a used-car dealer. The equipment would be from one to three years old when returned from the lease. All equipment is cleaned, repaired, and certified to meet original standards. While neither new nor the latest model, such equipment may meet the needs and requirements of the district for general purpose use. As with a program car purchase, the district would save significant amounts through the purchase of such equipment.

- Consider the purchase of used equipment that's been refurbished by a commercial reseller rather than an OEM. Such equipment is available from a variety of commercial resellers across the country.

- Consider a purchase of surplus equipment from a large organization or a government entity. Surplus equipment is not necessarily defective or obsolete but is equipment that's been removed from service because it's no longer needed or has been replaced by newer equipment. Many government entities have programs for dealing with surplus items. An example of one such program is found in Missouri. The state requires that all surplus technology equipment be transferred to its surplus property program and made available to all public entities in the state. You can find more information about this program online at **www.oa.mo.gov/purch/surplus.html**. Such programs exist for most states as well as the federal government. A Web search should provide the contact information you need to access such a program in your own state.

Once the selection, purchase, allocation, and installation of equipment is completed, the technology coordinator must see that an accurate technology inventory is established and maintained. An asset inventory provides critical information regarding what technology resources exist and how they are allocated. Inventory data are important to the technology planning process, budget planning, and decision making and provide the district organization information about long-term return on investment.

Management of the technology inventory can be challenging for organizations of any size and may prove especially complex for large organizations. A variety of software solutions are available to help technology coordinators and other IT professionals manage this complex and often frustrating task. ZENworks from Novell offers the technology coordinator the ability to gather asset inventory information through the district network. More information on this product can be found at **www.novell.com/products/zenworks**. Other solutions, such as Track-IT from Intuit, provide the tracking of technology assets through the network in addition to providing work-order management capabilities.

More information about the Track-IT series of products can be found at **www.itsolutions.intuit.com.**

How the technology coordinator chooses to manage the district inventory—manually, through an existing asset control system, or through one of the products mentioned here—is a matter of choice by the district. The critical issue is that the district technology inventory is established and kept up-to-date. This will prove important for technology planning, budgeting, E-rate applications, and the conveyance of information to district decision makers regarding the technology resources available in the district.

Ergonomics and Furniture Selection

When considering the purchase and installation of equipment, it's important the technology coordinator think carefully about ergonomics and about how using technology regularly will impact health. Computer equipment should never be set up on desks or tables intended for another purpose or activity. Desktop, chair, monitor, and keyboard heights should be carefully coordinated to minimize neck and eye strain and avoid hand and wrist injuries. The positioning of the mouse, the lighting, and the overall working environment should also be evaluated when setting up work areas. This attention to ergonomic details will help students and staff avoid both discomfort and the repetitive-motion problems associated with the use of technology.

Monitors should be installed at a viewing height comfortable for the user. The top of the monitor should be aligned with the user's eyes and should be 15 inches to 25 inches away from the user's head when sitting normally. It's important to minimize glare. If the classroom, lab, or office has windows, position computers so that they don't face them. Desks that have recessed monitors can be used in locations where the desks will be used for multiple purposes in addition to computing. The use of LCD or flat-screen monitors will help reduce the exposure to radiation that comes from a normal cathode ray tube (CRT) monitor.

If students will be using adjustable chairs designed for adults, it may be helpful to lower the armrests, raise the seat, and push the lumbar support forward. If chairs don't have these adjustments, you can place a pillow on the seat and behind the lower back. If feet dangle in this position, support them by providing some type of suitable footrest. Sitting perfectly upright isn't recommended; users should relax and keep slightly open angles while receiving proper support.

If students frequently work from papers or a textbook, consider using document holders. These allow books and papers to be placed closer to the monitor and in a more ergonomic angle. Positioning them close to the screen will minimize the need for users to turn and twist their heads while working.

It's also important that workstations have adjustable keyboard trays to accommodate users of various sizes. Arms should lie close to the body, not outstretched or reaching to the side; elbows should be at a 90-degree angle, or greater; and wrists should be neutral, i.e., at about the same level as forearms.

Other ergonomic considerations include the use of optical mice. These mice will require less maintenance and will prevent the theft or loss of mouse "balls."

Attention to such details will help students learn good work posture and avoid many of the problems associated with long-term office work.

Software Licensing and Installation

While the installation and setup of equipment is important, this equipment is of little use without an operating system and software programs appropriate to the needs of end users. As discussed in chapter 2, the technology coordinator will be concerned with the selection, purchase, and installation of a standard set of programs for each computer. The selection of a software suite ensures that all users will have access to the same tools. Whether the user sits down to use a computer in a classroom, lab, library, or office, the same programs will be available on machines in each of these areas.

Several options exist for the licensing of these programs. Some organizations may choose to purchase equipment that includes the software. The advantage here is that capital outlay funds, which normally cannot be used for the purchase of software alone, can be used to purchase a computer that has software preinstalled and rolled into the price of the machine. Other organizations may choose to license and install the programs separately from the equipment.

The choice for the organization depends primarily on what software packages they wish to have installed on the machines they buy and whether these packages are available as a standard option. If, for example, a district wishes to have Microsoft Office installed as a standard package and the software can be purchased already installed on a computer, it will save the district installation time and allow it to use capital outlay dollars. If the district wishes to install a package not available as a standard option, it may be necessary to either license the software separately and install it after delivery or set up a master machine and have the new equipment cloned. If the district chooses to install some of the many freeware or shareware programs available, then installation after delivery or working with the vendor to have the machines cloned are likely the only options.

helpful hint

Buying Consortiums

Software costs are a challenge for any school or district. An effective way to reduce licensing costs is to look for organizations or buying consortiums that allow the district to become part of larger purchasing blocs. For example, state contracts may offer opportunities for reducing software costs, particularly for common programs. Educational service centers may also offer programs to assist schools in this process. Service centers can use volume purchasing to secure a wide range of software packages at prices often unavailable elsewhere. Therefore, before buying from a commercial vendor, check pricing options available through a state contract purchase or a local educational service center.

In addition to looking at price options available through consortiums, technology coordinators should check to see what manufacturers are offering. Most manufacturers have academic licensing programs that make it relatively inexpensive for educational organizations to use their software. Such programs may offer licensing of specific numbers of machines at a particular cost per machine; alternatively, all computers throughout a building or district can be covered by a *site license* for a specific price.

Whatever the choice of the organization, it's important for the technology coordinator to ensure that an appropriate number of licensed copies have been purchased for all programs to be installed on school or district equipment.

Once software is selected and installed on district workstations, one of the challenges for the technology coordinator will be record keeping. Just as with equipment purchases, an accurate inventory of software installations should be established, and maintained at all times.

helpful hint

Home Use

Many software publishers offer those who have purchased district or building-site licenses the right to extend these licenses to teachers for their home use. Teachers who wish to work on school-related projects at home then enjoy the same software availability they have at school. This sort of licensing extension can be used for certain Microsoft products such as Office and is available from a variety of other publishers as well. Technology coordinators should check with their software vendors or contact publishers to find out if such a program exists for the product they intend to purchase.

Keeping track of the software versions installed in various locations to assure that a standard version is in use can be a very time-consuming task. It can also be quite challenging to track the number of licenses installed in order to comply with current licensing agreements. A wide variety of software utilities will assist the technology coordinator with this task.

One example of such a utility is the ZENworks software program available from Novell. This package provides a variety of tools to assist with the management of desktop computers used by an organization. For software management, ZENworks will provide reports on licenses currently in use on the network and also provide a detailed software inventory. This type of reporting can be critical in a large organization attempting to manage software installations in a variety of locations. More information about ZENworks features and capabilities can be found at **www.novell.com/products/zenworks**.

Help-Desk Support for Users

One of the most challenging tasks faced by technology coordinators is providing technical support to all users in the school or district. Teachers and staff members frequently need on-site and on-demand technical assistance, both with the equipment and software itself and with the implementation of the technology in the classroom. Standard and effective procedures must be in place for providing timely assistance to users and for solving software and hardware problems. Nearly two-thirds of all teachers polled in 2000 reported that lack of technical support or advice was a barrier to their use of technology (U.S. Department of Education National Center for Educational Statistics, 2000).

One method that has been used successfully in many industries is the establishment of a dedicated *help desk*. A help desk is a technical assistance center that can be contacted by phone or e-mail to get immediate help with technology-related questions or problems. When users encounter a problem, they place a call to a help-desk operator who has considerable experience with the hardware and software used by the organization. The help-desk operator will assist the user by answering questions, explaining procedures, or diagnosing problems. The operator first attempts to guide the user in solving the problem on his or her own. Help-desk operators might be members of the technology staff, or they may be members of a student technology support group, which have become increasingly common in schools across the nation.

If the creation of a help desk isn't possible, it's still important to establish consistent and responsive support procedures. By establishing procedures for requesting assistance and communicating them throughout the organization, technology coordinators can let teachers and staff members know what technical help is available and how to access it.

Small districts lacking the funds to create an actual help-desk staff position may rely on a help-desk e-mail address where users can send questions and requests for assistance. Recruiting teachers to serve as technology support contacts has worked in a number of schools across the country (Murray, 2001). Teachers who provide tech support and training may be given a reduced teaching load or paid extra in exchange for their help.

As mentioned above, students can also be a valuable resource in this regard. The Generation www.Y program is a good example. This program, started in 1996, prepares students to solve problems and assist teachers with the use of technology in the classroom. Students in the program pair up with a partner teacher to provide expertise with software and hardware, and they collaborate on the creation of learning projects that use technology. The program has been successfully implemented in many schools across the nation, and in 2000 it was recognized by the U.S. Department of Education as an exemplary program.

Other student technical-training programs exist for schools. The NetPrep program, sponsored by 3Com, is a program for secondary schools. This program is designed to introduce students to the basics of networking and prepare them for more advanced study after graduation from high school. The program consists of four semester-long courses covering networking fundamentals, *local area networks* (LAN), *wide area networks* (WAN), and network architectures. Students who complete this program are eligible for technical certification that may lead to employment after graduation. More information about this program can be found at: **www.3com.com/solutions/ en_US/education/programs/netprep_secondary.html**.

The Cisco Networking Academy is another technical-training program available to students. Launched in October 1997, the Networking Academy is now available in all 50 states. Academies are located in high schools, technical schools, colleges, universities, and community-based organizations. The academies provide technical training that leads to Cisco certification in networking skills. The academies have expanded to also include optional courses that provide training in Web design, PC hardware, and voice communication. More information about these academies can be found at the Cisco Academy Connection Web site: **http://cisco.netacad.net/public/academy/About.html**.

Technical assistance is also available through the Internet. Techs4Schools has created a Web site service that links teachers with information technology professionals who can provide advice and guidance. Educators who participate in this program are assigned to teams made up of IT professionals and classroom educators in need of support. The IT professionals come from a variety of backgrounds and can provide assistance with software and hardware issues, operating system questions and problems, networking, and

Internet usage. Questions are posed to the whole team via e-mail and answered in a timely fashion. While Techs4Schools is not intended to serve as a help desk, it can offer important assistance to educators by linking them to professionals who have expertise to share. To learn more about this program or to enroll as a participant, visit the Techs4Schools Web site at http://techs4schools.techcorps.org/about/index.shtml.

Equipment Repairs and Work Orders

While the help desk can be an important first line of support for end users, the time will come when a problem cannot be solved by telephone or e-mail and on-site technical assistance will be needed. When a desktop computer breaks down, it's important to return its functionality to the user as soon as possible so that work can be continued (McClure, Smith, & Sitko, 1997).

A system must be created to initiate this technical assistance and document the repairs necessary for a particular piece of equipment. Such a system can operate in a variety of ways. One district we're aware of asks users who need repairs to send an e-mail request to a special e-mail address (workorders@ourschool.org). A technology staff member monitors this e-mail account and either replies with information for users who may be able to solve the problem themselves or places the request on a schedule for a visit by a technician.

Other districts have created a paper document that's filled out and sent to the appropriate contact person at the building or district level. One of these districts uses a multipart form, and one copy goes to the technician, one goes to the scheduling secretary, and the third is kept as a record of services provided. Still other districts choose to have users file requests for service online through a special page on the school's or district's Web site. This type of electronic reporting allows for considerable information to be gathered regarding problems and solutions. Such a system also allows technicians to use any Internet-connected computer to check on reported problems and requests for service, thus reducing the time necessary to resolve the problem.

products can protect users from viruses that are spread through the broadcasting of e-mail messages containing infected files, it's also important to train users to follow basic rules of safe computing to avoid virus infection and other security threats. Network managers can mitigate these risks by setting up the e-mail server to filter out specific types of attachments (such as .exe and .cmd files), but users still must be trained to follow procedures such as saving and scanning attached files and programs before opening to avoid spreading viruses throughout the organization.

Another important security procedure is the backing up of critical data to removable media or a network resource. Training users to take the time to carry out a regular *backup* procedure will protect them from a variety of problems related to virus infection or machine failure. If regular backups of data are made, even if a virus infects a machine or the machine is compromised in some other way, critical information and work will not be lost.

While not technically viruses, *spyware* and *adware* are becoming considerable problems for IT departments in schools and businesses. These two types of programs collect information about the user, pop up annoying advertisements on the screen, steal *passwords*, and waste both network and workstation resources. These programs may be installed on a user's computer during a visit to a questionable Web site or through the installation of another program without the user's knowledge. Once installed, they can cause a variety of computer problems in addition to the gathering of user information.

Two excellent programs exist for identifying and removing this type of software: Ad-Aware from Lavasoft is a free program for removing adware and can be downloaded at **www.lavasoftusa.com**. Spybot Search and Destroy is a free program for identifying and removing a wide variety of spyware programs. Spybot can be downloaded from **www.safer-networking.org**.

Passwords can also be a security problem for those who manage computer networks. Users often choose passwords that are easy to remember but are also easy to crack by those who wish to gain illicit access to a computer network. Requiring users to change passwords on a regular basis will help avoid these problems. Educating users about good password procedures—such as choosing passwords that combine words, numbers, and symbols—will help keep networks more secure. Users should also be trained to never leave unattended computers logged onto the network; network managers can enforce this to some extent by setting the server to log off users whose workstations have been idle for a set amount of time.

To summarize: By having good anti-virus software in place and making sure the software is always current, a basic level of protection will be achieved for all school or district hardware. Training users to follow good security procedures will help keep virus infections to a minimum. Users must be made aware that they should not open e-mail messages from unknown users and should scan unexpected attachments for viruses before opening or saving. When users learn to consistently make backups of critical data and follow virus avoidance procedures, even a serious virus outbreak will not cause significant problems for the user. Requiring users to change passwords and teaching proper procedures for password creation and network use will help avoid unauthorized network access.

Equipment Maintenance and Upgrades

In addition to timely resolution of technical problems encountered by users, the technology coordinator must also be concerned with the regular maintenance and upgrading of equipment used by the organization. A regular, rigorous maintenance plan will allow equipment to remain trouble-free and operational as long as possible. This planned maintenance should include the regular update of virus protection files, cleaning and repair of peripherals such as mice and printers, and periodic maintenance of the hard disk to ensure maximum performance.

Mission-critical hardware such as servers and other network equipment should receive special maintenance and support consideration. The purchase of extended warranties to cover such equipment, and service contracts to support it when problems do arise, is a wise use of technology-support dollars. Such equipment should also be protected with uninterruptible power supplies that include battery-run backup capabilities. Such equipment will protect sensitive hardware from fluctuations in power and provide emergency power should a general service failure occur.

It's also important for the organization to have a long-term plan for upgrading equipment. As the memory and processing demands of new software and peripherals increase, it's often necessary to replace a computer's *CPU* or increase its memory to make use of the most recent software or operating system. It's a good idea, consequently, to establish guidelines for the planned upgrade of equipment.

Some districts may choose to phase out computers at the secondary level and transfer them to the elementary level when it's time to replace them with newer equipment. Others may wish to plan for the upgrade of equipment after a period of three years, with a maximum life expectancy of five years. It's useful to have the procedures for the upgrade and maintenance of equipment clearly defined in the district technology plan. This will help ensure that upgrades and eventual replacement of equipment at regular intervals will be built into the annual technology budget, and the process will be much smoother than if upgrades are done on an individual or haphazard basis.

equipment replacement guidelines

In considering the replacement and upgrade of existing technology equipment, the district will use the following information as an informal guide in determining the need for replacement until a formal replacement schedule is adopted:

Approximate Life Cycle of District Equipment

Desktop computers	*4 years*
Laptop computers	*3 years*
Computer monitors	*5–6 years*
Network printers	*Up to 8 years*
Serial printers	*Up to 10 years (if used by a single staff member)*
Flatbed scanner	*5 years*
Network servers	*3 years*
Network electronics	*2–3 years (rotation generally due to desire for increased speed/function)*
Digital cameras	*3–4 years*
Handheld palmtop devices and other PDAs	*Average 18 months (mostly due to damage)*
Televisions and VCRs	*6–8 years*
Video projectors	*6 years*
Overhead projectors	*12 years*
Video cameras	*3–5 years*
Computer cart	*10 years*

Adapted from *Technology Planning for Effective Teaching and Learning*, Steven M. Baule, 1999.

ANSWERS TO
Essential Questions

1 How can the technology coordinator assure that the purchasing, allocation, and inventory of equipment is carried out in an effective manner?

The technology coordinator should work with end users to develop the specifications for equipment to be purchased. School districts looking for ways to reduce hardware costs or maximize the purchasing power of their budgets should consider various purchasing strategies and sources. The technology coordinator should review the technology plan and consult with district and building leaders when making allocation decisions. A variety of software solutions are available to help technology coordinators manage the technology inventory and keep this critical information up to date.

2 What must the technology coordinator know about ergonomics and the selection of furniture for offices and classrooms?

The proper setup of technology equipment can have health benefits for users. Providing appropriate furniture and creating a comfortable work environment will help avoid user problems such as headaches and eyestrain.

3 What must the technology coordinator do to ensure proper licensing of software?

By keeping an up-to-date inventory of equipment and software and working with teachers and schools to purchase the required licensing agreements, the technology coordinator can ensure that software programs are properly licensed and installed.

4 How can the technology coordinator optimize help-desk support for end users?

Procedures must be created for providing technical assistance and support for users with questions or problems. Providing a central contact point for technology assistance and support will provide timely assistance to users and increase user comfort and satisfaction when using district technology resources.

5 How can the technology coordinator effectively protect computers from viruses, worms, and other security threats?

The technology coordinator must implement a multifaceted strategy for protecting technology resources. Network equipment and workstations must be protected from virus threats through the installation and regular update of anti-virus software. Users must be trained in proper procedures for avoiding problems with virus infection. It is also important to implement procedures to help district users avoid problems with spyware and adware. These procedures should include information and training about how to avoid the installation of these types of programs, as well as how to use tools that will allow for the easy removal of these programs.

6 What must the technology coordinator do to make sure equipment is properly maintained, upgraded, and repaired as necessary?

The technology coordinator must work with the school or district administration to establish plans for the necessary maintenance and replacement of equipment. An established plan for regular equipment upgrades will maximize performance and minimize the chances of equipment failure. A system for reporting problems, answering questions, and providing needed assistance and repairs must be established. Creating a set of standard procedures for requesting services and repairs will assure that problems are documented in a systematic manner and problems are resolved in a timely fashion. By implementing a standard reporting and tracking system for repair requests, it will also be possible to gather data about departmental performance. This data can be used in a variety of ways for technology planning and staffing considerations.

Resources

PRINT RESOURCES

Bateman, B. (2001). Maximizing your hardware investment. *Technology and Learning, 22*(3), 10-12.

Bateman, B. (2002). Installation made simple. *Technology and Learning, 22*(8), 46-48.

Carter, K. (2000). Staffing up for technology support. *Technology and Learning, 20*(8), 26-33.

Durost, R. A. (1994). Integrating computer technology: Planning, training, and support. *NASSP Bulletin, 78*(1), 49-54.

Foa, L., Schwab, R., & Johnson, M. (1996). Upgrading school technology. *Education Week, 15*(32), 40, 52.

Marcovitz, D. M. (1998). *Supporting technology in schools: The roles of computer coordinators.* Washington, DC: Society for Information Technology and Teacher Education Conference Proceedings. (ERIC Document Reproduction Service No. ED421150)

McClure, P. A., Smith, J. W., & Sitko, T. D. (1997). *The crisis in information technology support: Has our current model reached its limit?* Boulder, CO: Association for Managing and Using Information Resources in Higher Education CAUSE Paper Series #16. (ERIC Document Reproduction Service No. ED403837)

Murray, B. (2001). Tech support: More for less. *Technology and Learning, 22*(4), 40-44.

ONLINE RESOURCES

Association for Advancement of Computing in Education (AACE): **www.aace.org**

Consortium for School Networking (COSN): **www.cosn.org**

ERIC Clearinghouse on Information and Technology: **www.ericit.org**

Frisk Software International's F-Prot (an inexpensive anti-virus alternative to McAfee or Norton): **www.f-prot.com**

Grisoft's AVG (an inexpensive anti-virus alternative to McAfee or Norton): **www.grisoft.com/us/us_index.php**

International Society for Technology in Education (ISTE): **www.iste.org**

Intuit's Track-IT: **www.itsolutions.intuit.com**

Lavasoft's Ad-Aware: **www.lavasoftusa.com**

Microsoft Licensing Home: **www.microsoft.com/licensing**

Novell Worldwide Licensing Programs: **www.novell.com/licensing**

Office of Educational Technology, U.S. Department of Education: **www.ed.gov/Technology/index.html**

Software Spectrum Licensing Services: **www.swspectrum.com/licensing**

Spybot Search & Destroy: **www.safer-networking.org**

Techs4Schools, provided by TechCorps: **http://techs4schools.techcorps.org**

network operations

Essential Questions

1 How can the technology coordinator ensure that the network infrastructure meets users' needs?

2 How can the technology coordinator assist with the management of network user accounts?

3 How can the technology coordinator assist with the management of the district e-mail system?

4 How can the technology coordinator ensure that appropriate backup procedures are regularly carried out?

5 How can the technology coordinator use remote management tools to provide better network service and support?

6 What role should the technology coordinator play in the management of the district intranet?

The computer network of a school building or district has become the 21st-century equivalent of the human body's central nervous system. A network ties together the many different offices, classrooms, and other resources that allow the school to function effectively and provide quality educational services to students. A school network supports efficient e-mail communications, convenient access to database files, security for private documents and information, and access to shared resources such as printers and network-based programs. A computer network also makes it possible to take advantage of the information and resources that can be found on the World Wide Web.

A network has a variety of benefits for the technology coordinator. The network makes it possible to monitor and manage resources as well as staff and student usage. The tech coordinator can use the network to create for staff members a shared storage area that remains invisible to student users. Regular backups of both critical data and personal files are also possible. In addition, the network can be used to monitor the various devices and resources that are attached to the network.

A computer network also has a variety of advantages for staff and student users. A common storage area can be created so that staff or students can share documents and other information. Teachers can create a class folder on a shared network drive in which all students can save their work in individual folders. The files stored there will be automatically backed up on a regular basis and will be available to students in any location with network access: the computer lab, classroom, or library. The network makes it possible to work from many locations to access, share, and manage information.

The Internet has quickly become an almost indispensable resource for schools. It provides a wealth of information and makes it possible for students and teachers to learn in new and different ways. Access to a computer network and the resources of the Internet allows users to connect to information sources in their local area, in other states, or on the other side of the globe: "When students communicate with people in distant and foreign places they begin to understand, appreciate, and respect cultural, political, environmental, geographic, and linguistic similarities and differences" (Rogers, 1996).

The Web-Based Education Commission has called on legislators to "embrace an 'e-learning' agenda as a centerpiece of our nation's federal education policy" (U.S. Department of Education, 2000a). The federal government has also identified Internet access as a critical component of providing technology literacy for students. The first of five goals in the updated national technology education plan reads: "All students and teachers will have access to information technology in their classrooms, schools, communities, and homes" (U.S. Department of Education, 2000a). This means that establishing good network management plans and procedures must be a priority for all technology coordinators. By setting up quality network access, making sure the network is properly managed and administered, and providing the support and training necessary for all users, the coordinator can ensure that students, teachers, and other staff members have the resources they need to work and learn in our networked world.

Schools have made considerable progress with the implementation of networking projects and making Internet access available to teachers, students, and staff. The E-rate program has been a critical factor in this progress. The funds this program has provided for schools have allowed virtually all schools to be connected to the Internet and many of the schools to develop the network infrastructure necessary to deliver this access to classrooms. This access was one of the goals of the National Technology Plan developed by the Department of Education in late 1999 and early 2000. This plan and the complete report related to e-learning in our schools can be reviewed at **www.ed.gov/Technology/elearning/index.html**.

The National Technology Plan was instrumental in the building of infrastructure, the creation of Internet access, and the pioneering of ways in which digital content and networked applications could be used to transform teaching and learning. Following the plans of 1999 and 2000 was the passage of the No Child Left Behind Act of 2001, which has had implications for educational technology policy. NCLB charges the U.S. secretary of education with the development of the third National Technology Plan for education. This new plan will establish a national strategy supporting the effective use of technology to improve student academic achievement and prepare students for life and work in the 21st century. The development of this plan will provide an opportunity to reflect on the progress made in connecting classrooms to the Internet during a decade of increased federal, state, local, and private investments. The

Office of Educational Technology is developing this plan in conjunction with several organizations. More information about the plan can be found at **www.nationaledtechplan.org.**

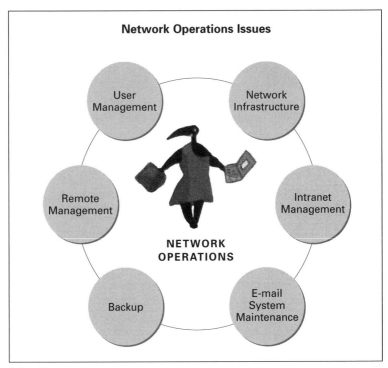

FIGURE 6

Network Infrastructure

The success of a school computer network is dependent on the design and durability of its infrastructure. The wiring, *patch panels,* file *servers, hubs, routers, print servers, high-speed communications lines* (such as *T1, T3,* frame-relay, and *fiber-optic lines*), wireless devices, and other parts of the network system must work together seamlessly to provide the services needed by end users. A poorly designed or maintained network will always fail at the worst possible moments.

Dealing with network infrastructure issues often requires highly specialized and advanced technical skills and knowledge. The technology coordinator may not be trained in all areas, but the coordinator should be willing and able to learn about them in order to plan and implement an effective network infrastructure and manage installations and upgrades. The school's or district's technology plan should include a detailed discussion of network resource needs and of the way infrastructure will be developed, expanded, and improved. The tech coordinator should work with school or district staff and the board of education, as well as outside vendors and consultants, to develop a network plan that will meet current and future curricular and administrative needs.

It's also important to plan for and secure adequate technical assistance for network equipment. A single person may not be able to handle server administration, user account setup, personnel training, equipment failures, and all the other requirements of network management. As a school's or district's network becomes more complex, the technology coordinator may need to work with administration to hire a certified network administrator: "The Technology Coordinator cannot do it all. Districts that have hired them and then become disillusioned because this person cannot oversee the whole thing, fix the problems and train the staff—there just aren't enough hours in the day" (Reilly, 1999). If the technology coordinator is the only person in the district responsible for technology, a plan must be in place for handling routine network maintenance and for repairing critical components

helpful hint

Tech Support

If additional technical support for the school's or district's network infrastructure is needed, provided below are a few ideas for securing that support:

- *Create partnerships with local businesses that have technical staff positions.*

- *Tap the expertise of the staff of local colleges.*

- *Contract with local vendors for regular and emergency technical-support visits.*

- *Work with existing custodial and maintenance staff to provide assistance as needed.*

- *Provide technical training for existing staff or hire additional staff with specialized technical training.*

- *Make use of parent volunteers who work in technical fields.*

- *Solicit help from a local technical school's computer-repair program.*

- *Recruit student helpers. They may have unexpected technical expertise and be able to provide useful assistance.*

when they develop problems or experience failure. A variety of service and support contracts are available from vendors.

Significant recent investment in technology infrastructure, often thanks to the E-rate program, has allowed many schools to install local area network (LAN) capabilities. Some technology coordinators, however, are still faced with the task of designing, installing, and configuring networks for their districts or particular buildings, or expanding the capabilities of an existing network. The tech coordinator planning to install or expand a network will be faced with a variety of issues and decisions. The networking needs of each organization are different; the network installed in one location may be quite different from that of another location, even in the same district. It's important to begin by considering what needs exist and how the network will meet those needs.

One of the first considerations must be the type of network to be installed. At one time, the only choice for installing network capabilities was to run wire to all the locations that would be connected to the network—essentially creating a hardwired network much like that of the telephone system. Copper wire would be installed connecting all the different connection points with a central location where the central network equipment (servers, routers, and switches) would be installed.

Today, it's possible to create an essentially wireless network by installing a minimum of wired connections throughout a building and then installing wireless access points that allow computers to connect to the network using radio frequencies. These wireless networks have become more reliable, faster, and less expensive in the last several years. In certain cases, they may be a better choice for installation than a hardwired network. In a newer building with false ceilings and easy access to conduit in walls, it may be possible to install a copper-wire network with minimal intrusion and nominal expense. In older buildings that have solid ceilings, it may be much more difficult and expensive to install a wire-based network throughout the building. The installation of a wireless network may be a better choice in such a location.

It's critical that a technology coordinator work with experienced technical experts to design and install the most appropriate network for a certain location. Some expertise may be available from staff with networking experience. Most schools, however, will need to engage contractors who will work with the coordinator and other technical staff to design and install the network.

For most schools, the LAN located in a school building will be connected to a larger network, either the district wide area network (WAN) or the Internet. When choosing how the school network will be connected to the outside world, the technology coordinator faces a variety of high-speed connectivity choices and issues. Schools can be connected through ISDN, T1, T3, broadband cable connections, or fiber optics. Each of these connection types has different speeds and costs.

ISDN connection. This digital transmission technology supports voice, video, and data-communications applications over regular telephone lines capable of speeds from 57.6 K to 128 K. Integrated Services Digital Network is a telecommunications standard.

T1 connection. This type of digital data connection can pass data at a rate of 1.544 megabits per second.

T3 connection. This type of digital data connection can pass data at a rate of 44 megabits per second. T3 lines are often used to link large computer networks, such as those that make up the Internet.

Broadband cable connection. This type of digital data connection, provided by a cable company, can reach speeds of up to 10 megabits per second.

Fiber-optic connection. This connection via a thin strand of glass that carries light transmissions is used for high-speed voice or data transmission. Fiber-optic connections can support 30,000 times the traffic that can be carried on copper wire.

Several factors need consideration when determining the connectivity scheme that works best for an organization or site. First will be the number of potential connections. Second will be what types of services will be delivered over the network. For example, a site that will be accessing video-on-demand services will need higher capacity and connection speeds than a site sending e-mail and browsing Web pages. The budget available will also be a factor to consider. Finally, the types of connections actually available must be determined, since connectivity service may vary from location to location.

To determine the best service option for providing network connectivity, it will be important for the technology coordinator to consult with the district's administration and business operations staff, network-services vendors, network design consultants, and other stakeholders.

User-Account Management

The success of any network is measured best by the end user's level of satisfaction and productivity. A network's infrastructure may be of the highest quality, but if the user has difficulty using the resources available, the network will not be viewed as a good investment of limited technology dollars. A user who is unable to log onto the network cannot access stored files, use network programs, visit a Web site, send an e-mail message, or make use of a network printer. Problems with a user account could cause a teacher who is uncomfortable with technology to abandon the network altogether—and lose all the many benefits it can offer. Effective management of user accounts is, therefore, crucial to network operations.

While technology coordinators may not be directly responsible for user-account management, it's important that they understand related issues and establish standard procedures for typical user-account problems, such as how to access accounts for new users, whom to contact when questions and problems arise, what to do when a password is forgotten, and how to help users access network resources that are of most use to them. These procedures should be specified and communicated to all users of the network so that when questions and problems arise people know what to do.

New-account requests and problems with passwords are part of the day-to-day management of any network. At the beginning of a school year it may be useful to work with administration and school offices to develop a list of new staff members who will need user accounts. These lists should serve as the basis for new-account requests. Lists of employees who have left the organization should also be developed so that those accounts can be removed. Password problems can arise at any time and need to be dealt with in a timely manner. Often these problems can be solved quickly by simply resetting a password that has been forgotten. It will be helpful for the technology coordinator or network administrator to designate a contact who can assist with these routine questions and problems. This person might be given some extra training and the authority to create new accounts and reset passwords as necessary.

Since training brand new users of the network so that they can access what they want and need is such an important aspect of the technology coordinator's job, a mandatory introductory class is good way to ensure that all new users receive a standard introduction to network use. This class can be offered at a variety of times and locations at the beginning of the school year. The session can be quite basic in nature and can be taught by the technology coordinator or technology contacts at school sites.

This mandatory class can be a useful way to help people learn how to connect to the network with user ID and password. A formal introduction to the network will help new users understand how the network is organized, such as public vs. private storage of files. It will help them learn what programs are available through the network, how to access such resources as the online library catalog, how to find out whom they can turn to when questions or problems arise, and so forth. This introductory class is also an ideal forum for introducing the district's Acceptable Use Policy (AUP) to new users.

Acceptable use policies are documents that outline the district's intended uses of the network and Internet. They set forth proper online behavior. The district's AUP should be one of the first policies developed when establishing a network and Internet connection. The technology coordinator is usually the staff member charged with formulating, implementing, and communicating this policy to other district staff.

Including the AUP in student handbooks ensures that all students and families will have a copy of the document and, therefore, the opportunity to review it before school activities begin. By having a document that is distributed to every user, the technology coordinator can educate users on potential pitfalls and provide guidance for students and parents. Some schools choose to have the AUP signed by both students and parents and kept on file in the office or classroom. This may be difficult for a large organization to do. The real purpose of such a document is to define boundaries of behavior and, more critically, specify the consequences of violating those boundaries.

Following are sample Acceptable Use Policy documents.

internet acceptable use policy

<Your> School District

INTERNET ACCEPTABLE USE AGREEMENT

Please read this document carefully before signing.

Internet access is now available to students and teachers in the <YOUR> School District.

We are very pleased to bring this access to <YOUR> School District and believe the Internet offers vast, diverse, and unique resources to both students and teachers. Our goal in providing this service to teachers and students is to promote educational excellence in schools by facilitating resource sharing, innovation, and communication.

The Internet is an electronic highway connecting thousands of computers all over the world and millions of individual subscribers. Students and teachers have access to:

1 Electronic mail (e-mail) communication with people all over the world.

2 Information and news from NASA as well as the opportunity to correspond with the scientists at NASA and other research institutions.

3 Public domain software and graphics of all types for school use.

4 Discussion groups on a plethora of topics ranging from Chinese culture to the environment to music to politics.

5 Access to many university library catalogs, the Library of Congress, and ERIC, a large collection of relevant information for educators and students.

With access to computers and people all over the world also comes the availability of material that may not be considered to be of educational value in the context of the school setting. <YOUR> School District has taken precautions to restrict access to controversial materials. However, on a global network it is impossible to control all materials, and an industrious user may discover controversial information. We (<YOUR> School District) firmly believe that the valuable information and interaction available on this worldwide network far outweigh the possibility that users may procure material that is not consistent with the educational goals of the district.

internet acceptable use policy

Page 2

Internet access is coordinated through a complex association of government agencies and regional and state networks. In addition, the smooth operation of the network relies upon the proper conduct of the end users, who must adhere to strict guidelines. These guidelines are provided herein so that you are aware of the responsibilities you are about to acquire. In general, this requires efficient, ethical, and legal utilization of the network resources. If a <YOUR> School District user violates any of these provisions, his or her account will be terminated and future access could possibly be denied.

The signature or signatures at the end of this document are legally binding and indicate that the party or parties who signed have read the terms and conditions carefully and understand their significance.

INTERNET—TERMS AND CONDITIONS OF USE

Acceptable Use. The purpose of the backbone networks making up the Internet is to support research and education in and among academic institutions by providing access to unique resources and the opportunity for collaborative work. The use of your account must be in support of education and research and consistent with the educational objectives of the <YOUR> School District. Use of another organization's network or computing resources must comply with the rules appropriate for that network. Transmission of any material in violation of any national or state regulation is prohibited. This includes, but is not limited to: copyrighted material, threatening or obscene material, or material protected by trade secret.

Privileges. The use of the Internet is a privilege, not a right, and inappropriate use will result in a cancellation of this privilege. (Each student or teacher who receives an account will be part of a discussion with a <YOUR> School District staff member pertaining to the proper use of the network.) The system administrators will deem what is inappropriate use and their decision is final. Also, the system administrators may close an account at any time as required. The administration, faculty, and staff of <YOUR> School District may request the system administrator to deny, revoke, or suspend specific user accounts.

internet acceptable use policy

Network Etiquette. You are expected to abide by the generally accepted rules of network etiquette. These include, but are not limited to, the following:

- Be polite. Do not get abusive in your messages to others.

- Use appropriate language. Do not swear or use vulgarities or any other inappropriate language.

- Illegal activities are strictly forbidden.

- Do not reveal your personal address or phone number, or those of students or colleagues.

- Note that electronic mail (e-mail) is not guaranteed to be private. People who operate the system do have access to all mail. Messages relating to or in support of illegal activities may be reported to the authorities.

- Do not use the network in such a way that you would disrupt the use of the network by other users.

- All communications and information accessible via the network should be assumed to be private property.

Warranties. <YOUR> School District makes no warranties of any kind, whether expressed or implied, for the service it is providing. <YOUR> School District will not be responsible for any damages you suffer. This includes loss of data resulting from delays, nondeliveries, misdeliveries, or service interruptions caused by its own negligence or your errors or omissions. Use of any information obtained via the Internet is at your own risk. <YOUR> School District specifically denies any responsibility for the accuracy or quality of information obtained through its services.

Security. Security on any computer system is a high priority, especially when the system involves many users. If you feel you can identify a security problem on the Internet, you must notify a system administrator or the <YOUR> School District Internet Coordinator. Do not demonstrate the problem to other users. Do not use another individual's account without written permission from that individual. Attempts to log on to the Internet as a system administrator will result in cancellation of user privileges. Any user identified as a security risk or as having a history of problems with other computer systems may be denied access to the Internet.

internet acceptable use policy

Vandalism. Vandalism will result in cancellation of privileges. Vandalism is defined as any malicious attempt to harm or destroy data of another user, the Internet, or any of the above-listed agencies or other networks that are connected to any of the Internet backbones. This includes, but is not limited to, the uploading or creation of computer viruses.

SCHOOL DISTRICT INTERNET USE AGREEMENT

I understand and will abide by the above Internet Acceptable Use Agreement. I further understand that any violation of the regulations above is unethical and may constitute a criminal offense. Should I commit any violation, my access privileges may be revoked and school disciplinary action, or appropriate legal action, may be taken.

User's Full Name: _____

User's Signature: _____

Date: _____

PARENT OR GUARDIAN

As the parent or guardian of this student, I have read the Internet Acceptable Use Agreement. I understand that this access is designed for educational purposes. <YOUR> School District has taken precautions to eliminate controversial material. However, I also recognize it is impossible for <YOUR> School District to restrict access to all controversial materials, and I will not hold the district responsible for materials acquired on the network. Further, I accept full responsibility for supervision if and when my child's use is not in a school setting. I hereby give permission to issue an account for my child and certify that the information contained on this form is correct.

Parent's or Guardian's Name: _____

Parent's or Guardian's Signature: _____

Date: _____

access acceptable use policy

<Your> School District

POLICY ON DISTRICT-PROVIDED ACCESS TO ELECTRONIC INFORMATION, SERVICES, AND NETWORKS

Freedom of expression is an inalienable human right and the foundation of self-government. Freedom of expression encompasses the right to freedom of speech and the corollary right to receive information. Such rights extend to minors as well as adults. Schools facilitate the exercise of these rights by providing access to information regardless of format or technology. In a free and democratic society, access to information is a fundamental right of citizenship.

In making decisions regarding student access to the Internet, the <YOUR> School District considers its own stated educational mission, goals, and objectives. Electronic information research skills are now fundamental to preparation of citizens and future employees. Access to the Internet enables students to explore thousands of libraries, databases, bulletin boards, and other resources while exchanging messages with people around the world. The district expects that faculty will blend thoughtful use of the Internet throughout the curriculum and will provide guidance and instruction to students in its use. As much as possible, district-provided access to Internet resources should be structured in ways that point students to resources which have been evaluated prior to use. While students will be able to move beyond those resources to others that have not been previewed by staff, they shall be provided with guidelines and lists of resources particularly suited to learning objectives.

When students are away from school, families bear responsibility for the same guidance of Internet use as they exercise with information sources such as television, telephone, radio, movies, and other possibly offensive media.

Students utilizing district-provided Internet access must first have the permission of, and be supervised by, the <YOUR> School District's professional staff. Students are responsible for good behavior online just as they are in a classroom or other area of the school. The same general rules for behavior and communications apply.

The purpose of district-provided Internet access is to facilitate communications in support of research and education. To remain eligible as users, students' use must be in support of and consistent with the educational objectives of the <YOUR> School District. Access is a privilege, not a right. Access entails responsibility.

access acceptable use policy

Users should not expect that files stored on school-based computers will always be private. Electronic messages and files stored on school-based computers may be treated like school lockers. Administrators and faculty may review files and messages to maintain system integrity and ensure that users are acting responsibly.

The following usage of district-provided Internet access is not permitted:

* uploading, downloading, or distributing pornographic, obscene, or sexually explicit material;

* transmitting obscene, abusive, sexually explicit, or threatening language;

* violating local, state, or federal statutes;

* vandalizing, damaging, or disabling the property of another individual or organization;

* accessing another individual's materials, information, or files without permission; and

* violating copyright or engaging in any other unauthorized use of the intellectual property of another individual or organization.

Any violation of district policy and rules may result in loss of district-provided access to the Internet. Additional disciplinary action may be determined at the building level in keeping with existing procedures and practices regarding inappropriate language or behavior. When and where applicable, law enforcement agencies may be involved.

The <YOUR> School District makes no warranties of any kind, neither expressed nor implied, for the Internet access it is providing. The district will not be responsible for any damages users suffer, including—but not limited to—loss of data resulting from delays or interruptions in service. The district will not be responsible for the accuracy, nature, or quality of information stored on district disks, hard drives, or servers, nor for the accuracy, nature, or quality of information gathered through district-provided Internet access. The district will not be responsible for personal property used to access district computers or networks or for district-provided Internet access. The district will not be responsible for unauthorized financial obligations resulting from district-provided access to the Internet.

access acceptable use policy

Parents of students in the <YOUR> School District shall be provided with the following information:

* The <YOUR> School District is pleased to offer its students access to the Internet. The Internet is an electronic highway connecting hundreds of thousands of computers and millions of individual users all over the world. This computer technology will help propel our schools through the communication age by allowing students and staff to access and use resources from distant computers, communicate and collaborate with other individuals and groups around the world, and significantly expand their available information base. The Internet is a tool for lifelong learning.

* Families should be aware that some material accessible via the Internet may contain items that are illegal, defamatory, inaccurate, or offensive to some people. In addition, it is possible to purchase certain goods and services via the Internet that could result in unwanted financial obligations for which a student's parent or guardian would be liable.

* While the district's intent is to make Internet access available in order to further educational goals and objectives, students may find ways to access other materials as well. Even should the district institute technical methods or systems to regulate students' Internet access, those methods or systems would not guarantee compliance with the district's Acceptable Use Policy. That notwithstanding, the district believes that the benefits to students of access to the Internet exceed any disadvantages. Ultimately, however, parents and guardians of minors are responsible for setting and conveying the standards that their children should follow when using media and information sources. Toward that end, the <YOUR> School District makes the district's complete Internet policy and procedures available on request for review by all parents, guardians, and other members of the community; and it provides parents and guardians the option of requesting for their minor children alternative activities not requiring Internet use.

NOTICE: This policy and all its provisions are subordinate to local, state, and federal statutes.

E-mail System Management

The school or district e-mail system is a vital network tool for all staff members. The e-mail system makes it possible to communicate with individuals and groups within the district; to send messages to parents, community members and vendors; and to interface with others outside the district.

Effective management of the e-mail system requires that procedures be established for creating new e-mail accounts and removing unused accounts. Users must know whom to contact when problems arise with their e-mail and where they can go to get assistance. A training program that covers how the system works, what features it provides, and how to make use of those capabilities is crucial for all users. E-mail systems today often provide a variety of features beyond the simple sending and receiving of messages, such as calendars for scheduling meetings, to-do lists, file sharing, and so forth.

In addition to sending e-mails to individuals, e-mail systems offer the ability to send messages to groups. If an e-mail system includes built-in group addressing, these addresses will need to be edited and updated as new people join a building or department and others leave. The school's or district's e-mail address book must be updated on a regular basis, both to ensure accuracy and to limit user frustration. While this task may be carried out by a network administrator, the technology coordinator should work with the administrator to ensure the accuracy of address book contents, coordinate communications with school administration regarding account management tasks, and coordinate training for new users.

When selecting an e-mail system for use by the organization, be aware that every system has its pros and cons. Essentially, two basic types of systems are available to choose from. An organization can either select a Web-based e-mail system (Yahoo and Hotmail are two examples of free Web-based accounts) or an e-mail system (such as Outlook or Eudora) that requires a local client. While both systems serve the same purpose of sending and receiving messages, each has advantages and disadvantages.

Although the technology coordinator may not be responsible for daily management of the e-mail system, a good understanding of how the entire system works and of the capabilities offered is certainly necessary in order to train users and help them take full advantage of the system, which in turn will result in satisfied users and a system that's easier to manage and maintain.

Backup Procedures

One of the most important procedures for ensuring network stability and integrity is the regular backup of files and information that network users access and modify. When a network file server is installed, the network administrator and technology coordinator must develop and implement a comprehensive plan for the daily backup of critical information. They must ensure that the necessary backup equipment and software are installed and working properly. The backup plan should also include disaster-recovery procedures to be used in the event of an attack on the system or its critical failure, so that vital data are not irretrievably lost.

Typically, files on the server are copied to tape in the early morning hours, when use of the system is minimal. After the backup is complete, the daily backup tape will need to be removed and stored, then replaced with the next day's tape. It's usually best to have a separate tape for each day of the business week. A designated person at each server location should be trained to switch the tapes on a daily basis.

helpful hint

Network Backups

Users should be trained to store all their important documents on the network. By doing so, they can be assured that their information will be backed up on a daily basis. This information can also be accessed from any computer attached to the network. Storing files on a local hard drive limits access to the computer where the files are stored and does not guarantee the regular backup of the information.

By training users in effective backup procedures, the technology coordinator will help users avoid losing critical data due to equipment failure or other unforeseen problems.

As part of the disaster-recovery plan, it will be important to send a copy of the tapes to an off-site location each week. By locating a copy of the tapes off-site, a disaster such as flood or fire will not destroy all copies of important files. As new tapes are sent for off-site storage, the original tapes can go back into the pool for daily backup.

An essential part of the backup plan is training users to save to the file server copies of important data and other files so that they can be backed up. Most desktop computers today have large quantities of local storage space, and users may not feel the need to store important files on the file server. Helping users understand the importance of backup and training them to make regular backups of critical information such as grades will help the backup plan succeed. Asking users to take a few minutes at the end of each work session to make a backup copy of important work will save later frustration. While computer equipment is often quite reliable, a single hard-drive failure with no backup can lead to the loss of important documents and information.

While technology coordinators may not be personally responsible for setting up and managing the backup system, they can play an important role in ensuring that the system is working properly. The backup system and software should be monitored on a daily basis to make sure that important files have been backed up successfully, that the backup is complete before users arrive in the morning, and that an adequate supply of backup tapes is available as needed.

Remote Management

Management of the network technology resources of a school district is a critical function that is usually handled by a small staff. Most districts will have multiple servers, often located in different buildings (and even different communities), that must be serviced and supported by a small staff or a single individual. A server that goes down at a particular site may be miles away from an available technician, and the time necessary to drive to the site to provide support may result in lost learning time or office staff productivity.

A district with multiple servers in various locations should seriously consider acquiring the tools and resources necessary to allow remote management of servers and network equipment via the Internet. These tools provide a variety of resources to network administrators and technology coordinators who are responsible for maintaining the integrity of the network and keeping the servers up and running.

Remote-management software tools for most types of network equipment are available from a variety of vendors. These tools allow a technician at a central location to monitor the operation of the network in multiple locations and report on the operating condition of devices such as servers, routers, and switches. When a problem is found with a piece of equipment, the technician is able to connect to the equipment from a remote site and take a variety of actions to resolve the problem. The technician may:

- Connect to the server console to complete diagnostics and access control software

- Reboot the server by recycling server power

- Recover or reinstall operating system software, applications, or user data

- Troubleshoot hardware problems

- Update drivers

- Install patches

- Manage rights, groups, and user accounts

The use of remote-management software tools offers a variety of advantages to those organizations willing to implement them. First, they can reduce the need for technical staff to personally visit a site to resolve network problems. Also, before an actual system failure occurs, it's possible to identify hardware components that are experiencing reduced performance and will need a scheduled replacement. Such tools can also warn of an impending server problem before it happens, leading to fewer service interruptions. While remote management will never be able to completely replace on-site support visits, a school district can use remote-management tools and capabilities to provide the best service possible to district users.

Intranet Management and Web Site Development

One of the many challenges that faces an organization is effective communication. Communication is enhanced when networks are created and connected to the Internet for sharing of resources and information and collaborating with others. Schools that want to more effectively share and communicate information often establish Web sites and intranets. Web sites contain information that is made available to the public, while intranets are essentially private Web sites that are usually restricted to internal use by an organization, such as a school district. The technology coordinator often plays a role in planning, establishing, developing, and managing district Web sites and intranets.

School districts often create private intranets to improve communication with staff. An intranet is one way to handle routine school administration issues and details. A private intranet available only to staff and teachers is an excellent place to publish such things as regulations, emergency procedures, human resources materials, and other relatively static information. A variety of paper-based forms can be published as files on the intranet and downloaded by district users to be completed for commonplace tasks. Publishing such forms on an intranet saves printing costs and allows information to be updated on a regular basis.

Since the technology coordinator will often be the central figure in the establishment and maintenance of a district intranet, it's important the coordinator work with district administration and school leaders to answer questions regarding it. For example:

- What do we want to accomplish by establishing an intranet?

- Who are the intended users of the intranet?

- What resources do we need?

- How will we maintain it?

The question regarding how the intranet site will be maintained is probably the most important one for the technology coordinator. It's essential to determine the procedures for maintenance at the outset: who will be responsible, how often the site will be updated, and how these updates will be posted to the site. It may be decided that regular maintenance will be the responsibility of staff members in the departments publishing information on the intranet site. If so, the technology coordinator must be sure they've received adequate training to do the updates and have the necessary software to complete the task.

By making sure regular maintenance of the site takes place, the district can be assured that important information is always up to date and readily available to employees.

ONE DISTRICT'S SUCCESS STORY

One district we're familiar with wanted to create a private intranet Web site for district personnel information and forms. Since the district already had a public Web site and server available, it created a new private intranet site on its public Web site and called it personnel.ourschool.org. The intranet site has a link on the personnel page of the public Web site, but it requires entering a user name and password to access the intranet site. A user name and password that were easy to remember were created and shared with all district staff. The new intranet Web site contains the following information:

- District personnel directory

- Work calendars for different employee groups

- Handbooks for different employee groups

- Insurance and benefit forms and information

- Certified staff salary schedule

- Miscellaneous payroll and leave forms

The intranet site is easy to access for any staff member, the district saves on printing costs for a variety of information and forms, and it's easy for the department to update information and forms at any time. A simple intranet solution saved this district time and money and makes information easy to access by those who need it.

ANSWERS TO
Essential Questions

1 How can the technology coordinator ensure that the network infrastructure meets users' needs?

The technology coordinator should work with administration and the board of education to create and carry out a network infrastructure plan that will meet the current and future needs of the school or district and achieve the goals of the technology plan.

2 How can the technology coordinator assist with the management of network user accounts?

The technology coordinator and the network administrator must work together to ensure that effective procedures are in place for managing network accounts and solving user problems. The technology coordinator must also plan and conduct training to help users understand the network and how to use it.

3 How can the technology coordinator assist with the management of the district e-mail system?

The most important role the technology coordinator will play here lies in the training of users to use the e-mail system properly and manage their own accounts effectively.

4 How can the technology coordinator ensure that appropriate backup procedures are regularly carried out?

The technology coordinator must work with the network administrator to ensure that a disaster-recovery plan is in place, equipment and software are appropriate for regular backups, and the system is monitored regularly. Users must also be trained to follow appropriate backup procedures for important files and data.

5 How can the technology coordinator use remote-management tools to provide better network service and support?

Remote-management tools can be used by the technology coordinator to solve network-related problems in a timely fashion, often without a site visit. These tools can also be used to constantly monitor the network for the purpose of diagnosing potential problems in order to maximize network performance and reduce service interruptions.

6 What role should the technology coordinator play in the management of the district intranet?

The technology coordinator should take a lead role in the planning, establishment, implementation, and management of the district intranet. Those who will regularly use the site to update information should be provided with the tools they need to do this and be trained in efficient methods of carrying out the updates.

Resources

PRINT RESOURCES

Brown, R. (1999). *Serving six institutions: A history of administrative computing at the Associated Colleges of Central Kansas.* McPherson, KS: Associated Colleges of Central Kansas. (ERIC Document Reproduction Service No. ED444414)

Harrington-Leuker, D. (2001). *New networks, old problems: Technology in urban schools.* Washington, DC: Education Writers Association Special Report. (ERIC Document Reproduction Service No. ED456188)

Hovenic, G. (1997). *Log on to the future: One school's success story.* Des Moines, IA: Iowa State Department of Education. (ERIC Document Reproduction Service No. ED419518)

Jensen, D. (2000). Creating technology infrastructures in a rural school district: A partnership approach. In S. DeWees & P. Hammer (Eds.), *Improving rural school facilities* (pp. 57-69). Collected papers presented at the National Working Conference on Improving Rural School Facilities, Kansas City, MO. (ERIC Document Reproduction Service No. ED445859)

Lamont, B. (1996). *A guide to networking a K–12 school district.* Unpublished masters thesis, University of Illinois, Urbana-Champaign.

New Mexico State Department of Education. (1995). *Educational technology institute report.* Santa Fe, NM: Author. (ERIC Document Reproduction Service No. ED460673)

Rogers, A. (1996). Living in the global village. *Electronic Learning, 13*(8), 28-29.

Son, T. (1998). *Network technology based application.* Portland, OR: Northwest Regional Educational Lab. (ERIC Document Reproduction Service No. ED417707)

ONLINE RESOURCES

Cisco Technical Assistance Center: **www.cisco.com/public/support/tac/home.shtml**

Consortium for School Networking: **www.cosn.org**

Florida Center for Instructional Technology, Educator's Guide to School Networks: **http://fcit.coedu.usf.edu/network/**

Microsoft Product Support Services: **http://support.microsoft.com**

Novell Customer Support: **http://support.novell.com**

Reilly, R. (1999). The technology coordinator: Curriculum leader or electronic janitor? *Multimedia Schools, 6*(3). Retrieved May 24, 2000, from **www.infotoday.com/mmschools/mmstocs/may99toc.htm**

The Schoolhouse Networking Operations Center: **www.ibiblio.org/cisco/noc.html**

U.S. Department of Education. (2000). *e-Learning: Putting a world class education at the fingertips of all children.* Retrieved November 22, 2001, from **www.ed.gov/Technology/elearning/e-learning.pdf**

U.S. Department of Education. (2000). *Falling through the net: Towards digital inclusion.* Retrieved December 13, 2001, from **http://search.ntia.doc.gov/pdf/fttn00.pdf**

U.S. Department of Education. (2000). *The power of the Internet for learning.* Retrieved December 20, 2000l, from **www.ed.gov/offices/AC/WBEC/FinalReport/**

administrative computing

Essential Questions

1 What must the technology coordinator know about the processing of such data as grades and other student records?

2 How can the technology coordinator assist with the management of human resources information?

3 How can the technology coordinator ensure that administrators have the technology resources they need to manage the school's or district's business operations?

4 What issues must the technology coordinator consider when implementing and supporting a system for *document imaging* and management?

A school district is an organization primarily concerned with teaching and learning, but it's also a business, and it uses technology to manage and streamline its business operations. This technology, called administrative computing, includes those systems and software programs that provide information-management and data-processing capabilities. The technology coordinator has an important role to play in the administrative-computing operations of the district.

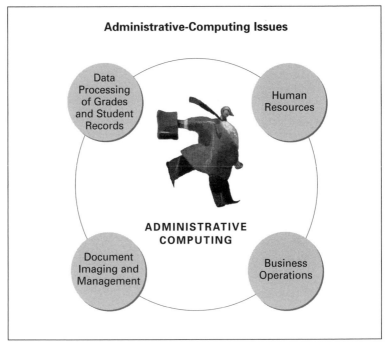

Administrative-Computing Issues

Data Processing of Grades and Student Records

Human Resources

ADMINISTRATIVE COMPUTING

Document Imaging and Management

Business Operations

FIGURE 7

Schools and districts use administrative-computing software in a number of ways: they create and manage student records, they set up master course schedules, they enroll students in those courses, and they develop systems of keeping personnel and business records. Schools in the district have a variety of information-processing and distribution needs, from the purchasing of classroom textbooks and supplies to the management of menus, meals, and other food-services provisions.

Technology coordinators should be prepared to understand and assist with these administrative-computing needs. They will need to work with administrators and office staff to develop technology solutions, consult with vendors about available products, and conduct staff development training sessions for business-software users. Through involvement in these activities, the tech coordinator can have a positive impact on the efficiency of a school's or district's business operations: "A well-planned information system in a school district significantly improves the ability of stakeholders to access data and efficiently make decisions" (Rodriguez, 1997).

Processing Grades and Student Records

Managing and processing information such as grades, student and employee records, and payroll figures are common administrative-computing tasks. This data processing occurs routinely in all schools and districts, and managing it is a recursive task for technology coordinators.

An administrative information system revolves around the management of these types of records. A variety of records will be created for every employee and student. They'll need to be updated and modified on a regular basis. The technology coordinator should work with administration to implement a system that adequately meets administrators' collection and reporting needs.

A centralized system usually offers advantages to a school or district with multiple buildings. By implementing a centralized system, student and employee records can be kept and maintained in one location, but they can be easily accessed by users throughout the organization. When a record is updated, the update is immediately available to all users of the system. If a school is using an information system that maintains records in separate locations, it's important to make sure all records are updated simultaneously so that current information is available to everyone.

The processing of data concerning grades is an ongoing administrative-computing function. Student information systems often include a component for managing grade information for transcripts and other student records. Until recently, the most common method for entering grade data was scanning bubble sheets filled out by teachers. Computerized grading programs have become more common and sophisticated, however, and they can now interface with student-information systems to either directly transfer grade information to the system or create files that can be imported on a regular basis. Accurate and up-to-date grade information is therefore much more easily gathered.

Numerous student-information systems have been developed by vendors for the K–12 educational market. Although some differences exist from product to product, certain basic features are included in all of them. Following are those needed in order to effectively manage student data for a school district.

toolbox tip

Master Family Record

One way to ensure that information about several students from the same family is updated at the same time is to establish a master family record in the administrative information system. This family record will contain all the basic information about the family: address, phone number, name of guardian, emergency contact, and so forth. When information is updated in the master record, all individual student records for that family will be updated simultaneously.

Student records. The ability to store information about each student enrolled in the district, such as address, phone number, name of guardian, emergency contact, and so forth.

Master schedule. The ability to create a master plan of classes and sections offered by a school.

Individual scheduling. The ability to enroll students in particular classes based on a master schedule developed by the school.

Grade reporting and records. The ability to create progress reports, grading-period reports, and transcripts.

Attendance. The ability to provide student and class-attendance records needed for state reporting by the school or district.

Reporting. The ability to generate a variety of reports based on the data in the system. With the increased requirements of the No Child Left Behind Act, this feature should be robust and provide a great deal of flexibility.

The variety of other available features, as well as add-on components that extend them, include the ability to post, on a protected Web site, assignment information and grades. Parents and students can log on to these protected sites and view these data. A growing number of schools are choosing this feature. Some vendors include it as a standard part of the package, while others market it as an add-on component.

Other add-on packages and components include special-education record keeping and IEP tracking, fee management, and textbook rental and inventory tracking. Additional products can be purchased to work in conjunction with the student-information system to provide teachers improved assessment and tracking standards as an aid in instructional management.

All of these basic features can be found in such programs as SASIxp, from Pearson Education (**www.pearsondigital.com/sasi**); the MacSchool or WinSchool products, from Chancery Software (**www.chancery.com/products.html**); or PowerSchool, from Apple Computer (**www.apple.com/education/powerschool**). All of these products provide the necessary tools and features to manage student information and have been used successfully by a number of schools.

When selecting a student-information system and a grade-management program for use by teachers, the technology coordinator, IT staff, administration, and project planning committee should make sure the programs integrate well with one another and that the data transfer between programs is simple and accurate. If the feature that allows students and parents to log on to a protected Web site to view grade and assignment information is contemplated, careful attention should be paid to data security, equipment requirements, and teacher concerns about such a feature. It's important to note that permission must be obtained from parents if student data are to be posted online. It's also important to consider that while such a system may make it possible to post student scores and grade data on the Internet, this can lead to unreasonable expectations that this information should be posted immediately, which is not always possible or even desirable. Therefore, such a feature should be implemented only after weighing the pros and cons and after appropriate administrative policies have been developed and put into place.

The technology coordinator will play an important role in training users to implement the information-management system. Users need to understand how the system works and how they can use it to perform their jobs more effectively. They must know how to get assistance when they have questions or encounter problems. Although the system may be maintained by IT staff or supported by outside vendors, the tech coordinator must coordinate their efforts so that staff members have ready access to the data and information they need for decision making: "Those districts willing to take the plunge to build sustainable information-management systems are likely to reap many benefits" (Rodriguez, 1997).

Human Resources

The management of human resources records is another area of administrative computing that technology coordinators are likely to be involved in. Information-management systems used for student records can often be used for employee records as well, tracking such details as salaries, wage and hours, benefits, and supplemental contract agreements.

Technology coordinators can play a significant role in supporting the school's or district's human resources function by working with HR in analysis and planning regarding technology purchases and implementation. Coordinators can work with vendors to select the appropriate hardware and software, and they can provide training and ongoing support for users.

Implementing an HR information-management system can be a complex and time-consuming undertaking. A struggle that a nearby school district was having with a particular aspect of its HR information system provides us with a real-world example of how a district might go about implementing a new system. Let's take a look at the procedures the district followed to improve this aspect of information management.

The district began by organizing a team made up of the technology coordinator, staff from district administration, and staff from the personnel and business offices. The team began by reviewing current procedures and establishing goals for the project.

Team members found that current hourly record keeping was done on paper time cards. Every month, two payroll staffers spent 20 hours overtime apiece resolving and correcting time-card errors and questions. When processing yearly contract renewals, three people entered teacher contract information by hand in three different systems.

In meeting and reviewing this information, the team established goals for implementing an entirely new system. The most desirable one would use electronic time clocks to enter data directly into the payroll system. Contract information would be easily shared between different offices and systems that needed access to the data.

Once the goals for the project had been established, the technology coordinator contacted various vendors, providing them with a project description and requesting an informational product presentation. The team spent nearly six weeks viewing product demonstrations, comparing system features, and gathering additional information. The purpose of these informational sessions was to compare products and select several vendors from which to secure bids.

After the long list of possible products had been narrowed, the technology coordinator worked with the purchasing department to develop a request for proposals from vendors. This document described the district project, outlined the project goals, and requested a proposal from each vendor specifying how the vendor might design a complete solution and the cost. Requests for proposals were sent to four of the vendors who had presented informational sessions. The team also spent time developing an evaluation process to help with the rating of proposals, including project scope, timeline for completion, how well the product met the project criteria, and the cost of the solution.

Each of the proposals was evaluated by the team according to the pre-established criteria. Ultimately, a single vendor was selected to provide the system and was contacted to meet with the team to begin detailed project planning. Timelines were developed and communicated to district schools and staff. It was decided that the implementation of the electronic time clocks would be rolled out in phases, beginning with two sites and expanding, in phases, to all sites.

As the system was being installed at the district office site, initial user training took place for those who would directly use the new system to manage information on a daily basis. As the two pilot sites came online, various problems were discovered, repairs and changes made, and procedures refined. As the district prepared to bring additional sites online with the time clocks, more users were trained to use the new system. Within a period of four months, all district sites were online.

After the completion of the project, the team continued to meet for several months to review progress and identify the benefits of the new system. Feedback from office employees indicated that processing of hourly employee data for payroll was no longer requiring overtime. Hourly employees indicated they liked having leave and vacation data available to them whenever they accessed the time clock system. Contract information was flowing much more efficiently between offices and systems.

In this case, the technology coordinator was able to provide important leadership and assistance in facilitating a project to benefit district staff and improve the management of information. By using a simple seven-step process, problems with the current human resources system were addressed and procedures improved to the satisfaction of both the district staff and the employees. These seven steps were review, set goals, gather information, get proposals, plan project, implement carefully, and evaluate progress.

The technology coordinator can also assist with employee recruitment by implementing a system for posting job opportunities on the district's Web site as well as other employment sites. Postings can be placed with university placement offices. States offer online job listings as well, such as the Kansas Education Employment Board (**www.kansasteachingjobs.com**) and the Florida Official Teacher Recruiting Web site from the Florida Department of Education (**www.teachinflorida.com**). National listings such as the Clearinghouse for School Positions in the USA (**www.wanttoteach.com**) or the Regional Educational Applicant Placement Web site (**www.reap.net**) are also good places to post openings. By listing job opportunities on these sites, the school or district will have a better chance of hiring highly qualified candidates for open positions.

Business Operations

Purchasing is an important part of a school's or district's daily operations. The business office must generate purchase orders, track the filling of these orders, acknowledge the receipt of merchandise, manage the inventory of district assets, and arrange for the payment of accounts. In addition, the district is often required to generate requests for proposals and bids involving large purchases, then manage the bidding process to award contracts.

While business officers usually manage these purchasing operations, the technology coordinator will often play a role in supporting the technology they use. This technology usually takes the form of a centralized information-management system. Such a system may be an add-on component of the student information-management system, or it may be separate. An example of such an add-on would be the CIMS GT Financial software program, which can be integrated with other information-management products such as SASI, from Pearson Education (**www.pearsondigital.com/cims**). This suite of programs includes components for managing purchasing and receiving, fixed assets, and warehouse inventory. A variety of stand-alone accounting packages are available for schools and nonprofits.

It's the responsibility of the technology coordinator to be sure that appropriate technology resources—such as connectivity, workstations, and training for users of key programs—are available to business office staff. For example, to access the information-management system effectively, all offices must have the necessary network connections. In addition, office staff who spend eight hours a day working with purchasing or accounting data may need workstations with computer monitors of 19 or 21 inches to help avoid eyestrain. Also, workers will need to be trained in the daily operation of the workstation and software they use.

The effective use of technology to support the purchasing operations of a school or district will result in better financial management. Through the use of an information-management system, the school or district will have better access to financial data and other critical information necessary for decision making, as well as be able to make better use of the resources available to them.

Document Imaging and Management

School districts, like many other organizations, generate a huge number of paper records as part of their day-to-day operations. Management of business records, student records, transcripts, student portfolios, required reports, and other paper documents has become a major challenge for many organizations. Records must be maintained in accordance with state and federal law, as well as the record-keeping and business needs of the school or district itself. The technology coordinator can help streamline this task by planning and implementing a system for document imaging and management.

Document imaging is the conversion of a paper document into an electronic image that can be accessed by a computer. Once a document has been converted into an image and stored in the system, it can be retrieved quickly and efficiently. An imaging system is made up of several separate elements, all of them important. These elements include scanning, storage, retrieval, indexing (creating a system for document filing), and user access.

In considering a document-management system, the two most critical elements are the storage and retrieval processes. Many different types of scanners are available, and they're capable of scanning anywhere from a few pages per minute to several hundred. Conducting a careful needs analysis as part of initial planning will help determine the number and types of scanners needed and where these scanners should be located.

A variety of storage options are available. Most organizations will benefit from recording information on some kind of optical drive and using a jukebox device to distribute and arrange information on several different discs.

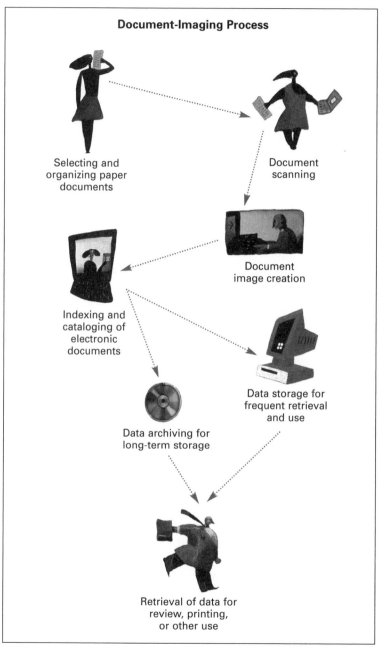

Document-Imaging Process

Selecting and organizing paper documents

Document scanning

Document image creation

Indexing and cataloging of electronic documents

Data storage for frequent retrieval and use

Data archiving for long-term storage

Retrieval of data for review, printing, or other use

FIGURE 8

Document-management software can be used to organize and index the documents so that they can be retrieved easily. Documents can be indexed in several ways: fields and keywords indexing, full-text indexing, or a file or folder system. Good document-management software will allow information to be indexed in a variety of different ways at the same time so that users can easily retrieve needed information regardless of how they search for it. Some users may wish to retrieve information by keyword, while others need to find documents through the use of full-text searches.

The final component of the system is control of access to the *archived* documents. An imaging system must provide users with easy access to the information they need while at the same time restricting access to sensitive information that's not within their purview. Some users will need access to student records, others to employee files, while still others will need to access business records stored in the system. The system must be flexible enough to meet all these different needs without compromising security.

A variety of important questions must be asked when planning and establishing a document-imaging system that will meet the district's document-management needs. Among them are the following:

- What problems will this system solve and how will the system improve the productivity of the organization?

- How many documents will the system store, and for what purpose?

- How many users will need to use the system at the same time?

- Which offices will need access to the system, and where are the users located?

- Is the necessary network connectivity available for users of the system? Is this connectivity adequate for the system's successful use?

For some districts, the planning, purchase, implementation, and support of a document-imaging system will be a viable project. For others, the implementation of such a system may be out of the question due to budget constraints, lack of staff to install and support such a system, or limited return on investment due to the size of the district.

For those districts that do want to implement such a system but have limited resources to do so, outsourcing may be a possible solution. Outsourcing document imaging can provide electronic storage and access to information and documents while avoiding the up-front costs of acquiring and supporting such a system. This is a possibility that must be explored when considering the implementation of an imaging and management system for the district's documents.

By working with administrators and office staff to determine the answers to the questions above, the technology coordinator can design a document-management system that meets user needs. The coordinator will then need to work with vendors to select the appropriate hardware and software, plan the installation of the system, create a training program for users, and address issues of system administration and ongoing support.

The successful planning and implementation of a document-management system can have many benefits for a school district. Archived documents are more easily accessed by users, thus increasing productivity. Document access can be more easily regulated, ensuring employee- and student-record confidentiality. Records are readily available precisely when they're needed. Principals, for example, can review employment applications on their desktop computers rather than visiting the personnel office to review them. A document-management system can also save considerable space in the storage of archival files, and electronic documents can become part of a disaster-recovery plan. Archived records can be copied and stored offsite to allow the re-creation of the data archive system should a disaster occur and destroy the paper records of the organization.

While administrative computing may not be the chief focus of the technology coordinator's job, the leadership, support, and guidance that tech coordinators can bring to these activities will help ensure the success of the organization and maximize the return on investment in technology in support of a school's or district's business operations.

ANSWERS TO
Essential Questions

1 What must the technology coordinator know about the processing of such data as grades and other student records?

The technology coordinator should have a detailed understanding of the system used to manage grades and student information in order to provide training and offer assistance to users of this system. All those who work with students and grades will need this training and assistance.

2 How can the technology coordinator assist with the management of human resources information?

In addition to user support and training on the information-management system, the technology coordinator should be prepared to assist with the posting of employment opportunities to various Web sites in order to attract quality teacher candidates and applicants for other positions.

3 How can the technology coordinator ensure that administrators have the technology resources they need to manage the school's or district's business operations?

In supporting the purchasing process for a district, the technology coordinator must ensure that users have the workstations, software resources, network connectivity, training, and support they need to perform their jobs efficiently.

4 What issues must the technology coordinator consider when implementing and supporting a system for document imaging and management?

In implementing a system for document imaging and management, the technology coordinator must discuss the documentation needs and overall scope of the system with administrators and staff, work with vendors to select the appropriate hardware and software, and develop a comprehensive plan for successful training and support of system users.

Resources

PRINT RESOURCES

Anderson, R., & Dexter, S. (2000). *School technology leadership: Incidence and impact.* (National Survey Report #6). Irvine, CA: Center for Research on Information Technology and Organizations. (ERIC Document Reproduction Service No. ED449786)

Carter, D. S., Kelly, P., & Connors, M. (1996). *Implementing an instructional information management system in a catholic secondary school.* Paper presented at the National Conference of the Australian College of Education, Perth, Australia. (ERIC Document Reproduction Service No. ED413632)

Hallman, T. (1995). *Getting everyone into the tent.* Association of Small Computer Users in Education Conference Proceedings, Myrtle Beach, SC. (ERIC Document Reproduction Service No. ED387098)

Hoffman, R. (2002). Strategic planning: Lessons learned from a "big-business" district. *Technology and Learning, 22*(10), 26-38.

House, J. (1989). *The impact of personal computing on the educational administration knowledge base.* Education Writers Association Special Report, Washington, DC. (ERIC Document Reproduction Service No. ED456188)

ONLINE RESOURCES

Clearinghouse for School Positions in the USA: **www.wanttoteach.com**

CIMS GT Financial Programs, from Pearson Education: **www.pearsondigital.com/cims**

Electronic School: **www.electronic-school.com**

Florida Official Teacher Recruiting: **www.teachinflorida.com**

Johnson, D., & Bartleson, E. (1999). Technological literacy for administrators. *AASA School Administrator Web Edition, April 1999.* Retrieved July 17, 2002, from **www.aasa.org/publications/sa/1999_04/johnson.htm**

Kansas Education Employment Board: **www.kansasteachingjobs.com**

LaserFiche Basics for Document Imaging and Management: **www.laserfiche.com/basics/index.html**

MacSchool or WinSchool, from Chancery Software: **www.chancery.com/products.html**

NCS Imaging Products and Solutions:
www.pearsonncs.com/imaging/index.htm

PowerSchool, from Apple Computer: www.apple.com/education/powerschool

Regional Educational Applicant Placement: www.reap.net

Rodriguez, J. (1997). Building an adaptive information system. *AASA School Administrator Web Edition, April 1997.* Retrieved July 17, 2002, from www.aasa.org/publications/sa/1997_04/rodriguez.htm

SASIxp, from Pearson Education: www.pearsondigital.com/sasi

Student Information Systems Demystified:
www.techlearning.com/story/showArticle.jhtml?articleID=19400338

Virtual Schoolhouse: www.ibiblio.org/cisco/schoolhouse/

budgeting and planning

Essential Questions

1 What should the technology coordinator know about developing a comprehensive and successful technology plan?

2 How can the technology coordinator assist administrators in creating and carrying out a sound technology budget?

3 How can the technology coordinator assist in evaluating the effectiveness of technology use in the school or district?

4 What does the technology coordinator need to know about grant writing to locate and secure additional funding for technology projects?

5 What should the technology coordinator know about the E-rate program and application process?

The primary function of a technology coordinator is to serve as the technology leader for the school or district. The importance and challenge of this leadership role are most evident in the areas of budgeting and planning.

The technology coordinator can best fulfill this role by articulating a vision for technology use in the school or district; establishing a clear, achievable plan for making that vision a reality; and working with administrators and the board of education to find the resources necessary to make it all happen. By developing a comprehensive and appropriate technology budget, securing grants and other outside funding to move big programs forward, and applying for discounts and refunds from the E-rate program, the tech coordinator can have a tremendous impact on the successful implementation of technology in the school or district.

FIGURE 9

Technology Planning

Over the past 20 years, schools have spent vast sums of money purchasing technology for classrooms and offices. While this spending shows a dramatic increase in technology investment, there's often been a lack of essential planning regarding what purposes the technology would serve and how it would be used to accomplish those purposes. The expectation has commonly been that simply placing technology tools in the classroom leads to exciting results and improved student learning.

However, any school or district that wants to make sure technology expenditures have the intended impact for students and staff must have a carefully developed technology plan. This plan represents a three- to five-year road map of where the school or district wishes to go with technology. It also represents the results of many conversations among board members, administrators, teaching staff, and people in the community regarding how technology can support the learning process and how pedagogy and the learning environment must change in order to make better use of the tools available and provide richer experiences for students. The technology coordinator plays an important role in fostering and sustaining these conversations

Most schools and districts today do develop technology plans. In fact, districts are often required to submit a plan to the state for approval, particularly if E-rate funding is involved; in order for a school to be eligible to receive E-rate funding, its technology plan must have been approved by the state or some other organization charged with reviewing and approving such plans.

In the past, plans often concentrated on the acquisition of hardware or the development of network infrastructure. While these components are important, an effective technology plan encompasses much more. Barnett (2001) has defined 10 essential elements of a successful technology plan:

- Create a vision

- Involve all stakeholders

- Gather data

* Review the research

* Integrate technology in the curriculum

* Commit to professional development

* Ensure a sound infrastructure

* Allocate appropriate funding and budget

* Plan for ongoing assessment and monitoring

* Prepare for tomorrow

The list above comprises the basic components necessary for the development of a technology plan.

The National Center for Technology Planning, Dan Lumley and Gerald Bailey at Kansas State University, and the Regional Technology in Education Consortia are a few of the sources that can provide a variety of models and approaches for planning technology. Founded by Dr. Larry Anderson in 1992, the National Center for Technology Planning (**www.nctp.com**) serves as a clearinghouse for information. The Web site makes available a wide range of plans from schools and districts across the nation. It also contains articles, brochures, checklists, and other items to assist in the planning process. While many of the resources on the site are free, the site does sell such selected items as audiotapes and a guidebook. Other services include coaching, consulting, and workshops.

It might also be beneficial to consult some of the online resources available before beginning the process of developing or updating a technology plan. For example, The STaR (School Technology and Readiness) chart developed by the CEO Forum is one tool technology coordinators can use. It's found at **www.iste.org/starchart**. The STaR chart is a self-assessment tool intended to help schools integrate technology. When a school answers a series of online questions, it receives feedback about its progress. Its profile is compared with the profiles of four schools that have little technology, then with profiles of four schools considered to be models for the innovative use and integration of technology. While the chart is not intended to be used for evaluation purposes, the feedback can help the school decide if technology is being used effectively and what areas need to be focused on to improve technology integration.

NCRtec (North Central Regional Technology in Education Consortium) has created a resource site for technology planning at **www.ncrtec.org/capacity/guidewww/gqhome.htm**. This site offers a series of questions for technology planning and includes planning models and reference materials. The questions provide guidance on such larger issues as how to determine the vision for learning, how to support the vision with technology, and how to gain public support for the vision. They are also designed to create discussion within the technology planning team that will help them make informed decisions about what should be contained in the technology plan.

The International Society for Technology in Education (ISTE) has created the Technology Support Index (**http://tsi.iste.org**) to help schools plan and provide support systems to enhance the use of technology in education. The index was developed both to identify support strategies used effectively in exemplary districts and to provide tools districts can use to improve technology support services. The index identifies four domains of technology support: equipment standards, staffing and processes, professional development, and intelligent systems. The site offers an online assessment tool for identifying each domain's strengths as well as the areas needing improvement. While not intended to be an in-depth program evaluation, the index can serve as a useful starting place for understanding the importance of effective technology support.

The technology coordinator needs to enlist the aid of a variety of stakeholders when beginning the planning process. By involving teachers, administrators, board members, community representatives, and students, a wide range of ideas can be expressed and vetted and a broad base of support for the plan can be established. The coordinator should work with these stakeholders to develop a vision statement that defines what the technology program will look like in three to five years. The statement should include how students and teachers will be using technology to support and enhance the learning process.

No planning process can be effective without data to support decision making. The technology coordinator must provide the planning group with up-to-date information about the school's or district's technology inventory, that is, the equipment and software currently used in classrooms, labs, and media centers. It's also a good idea to conduct a systemwide survey of technology usage by teachers and students and report the results to the group. Information about how other districts are making good use of technology can also be shared. Arranging site visits so that stakeholders can see how teachers and students in other schools are using technology in novel and compelling ways is an excellent way to raise awareness and interest.

helpful hint

NETS

One way to emphasize the importance of ongoing staff development for schools is to familiarize the planning committee with the National Educational Technology Standards (NETS) developed by the International Society for Technology in Education.

The NETS project developed standards for K–12 students, teachers, and administrators. Linking plans for staff development to the standards for teachers and administrators will result in more effective technology integration practices. More information about NETS can be found at www.iste.org/standards/index.html.

The technology planning committee will benefit immensely if members are given access to current research on the use of technology in learning. The technology coordinator should consider creating a summary review of the literature, identifying and locating articles that are particularly appropriate for the task at hand and sharing that information with the planning committee. By emphasizing current research on learning effects, the technology coordinator can help focus the committee's planning efforts. The focus should be on how to integrate technology more successfully into the curriculum rather than on hardware specifications, software titles, or network infrastructure. Powerful computers, the latest software, and high-speed access to the Internet are great, but they're not enough by themselves to ensure successful technology integration. Enhanced student learning should always come first when creating or revising a technology plan.

The component most often missing from a school's or district's technology plan is the allocation of resources for professional development and training. While considerable attention is often paid to the purchase and upkeep of equipment, the need to train teachers and staff to effectively use that equipment is often overlooked—a critical mistake. The technology coordinator must be sure that an ongoing staff development program is included as an integral part of the technology plan. Failure to include this element, or an emphasis on one-time-only opportunities for staff development, will make the success of the plan much more elusive. It's also important to note that one of the changes required by the No Child Left Behind Act is an emphasis on long-term, sustained staff development in a variety of areas, including the use of technology for learning.

The technology plan must also address technical support and infrastructure needs. The technology coordinator is usually responsible for identifying those needs and drafting a budget that will support them in a stable and sustainable way. Too often, funding in the past has been haphazard, relying on funds left over at the end of the year or other "soft" money, such as grants. For some organizations, this has led to questionable purchasing decisions that have suffered from lack of ongoing support. By working with the board and administration, the tech coordinator can make sure necessary financial supports are in place to carry out all components of the technology plan.

No technology plan is complete without an evaluation component: staff, teacher, and student use of technology must be regularly monitored and assessed for progress. The technology coordinator should assist in developing and administering surveys, defining learning outcomes, and implementing evaluation *rubrics* throughout the school or district. The information gathered from these assessments should be compiled and shared with stakeholders for further analysis and use in future planning. In order to stay on top of exciting new developments in technology that may improve learning outcomes, the tech coordinator should also regularly spend time reading about new products and developments, attending conference presentations, and discussing products with vendors

As you can see, a technology plan is much more than a shopping list of hardware and software needs. It's a comprehensive plan that includes a variety of critical components that, taken together, will "provide the necessary information to address not only technology but school improvement needs, and will provide the programmatic support necessary to sustain this project over time" (New York State Education Department, 1996).

Budgeting

Providing and supporting technology requires considerable financial commitment from a school district. In order for a technology program to be successful, the technology coordinator and administration must ensure that an adequate budget is available to provide the necessary equipment, software, connectivity, repairs, support, and training. While few businesses would ever try to implement a technology program without at least a minimal budget for it, school districts have been known to attempt to start them without identifying and obtaining adequate financial resources. The technology coordinator must make sure this does not happen; money must be allocated in each budget cycle for hardware, software, maintenance, telecommunications services, miscellaneous supplies, and professional development.

By budgeting carefully; assessing administrative, curricular, and infrastructure needs; and working with the board of education and administration to develop funding that adequately meets those needs, the technology coordinator can ensure that the school or district technology plan is suitably funded and sustainable.

Building an effective budget can be a time-consuming process for the technology coordinator. Considerable time can elapse from the initial needs assessment to the actual approval of a budget; therefore, the earlier the start, the better the outcome. While each district will have a budgeting process that's unique to that organization, some common themes can be recognized.

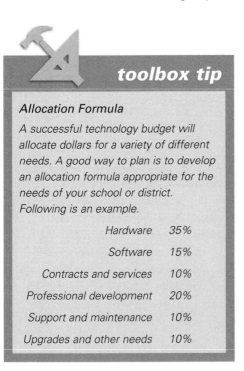

toolbox tip

Allocation Formula

A successful technology budget will allocate dollars for a variety of different needs. A good way to plan is to develop an allocation formula appropriate for the needs of your school or district. Following is an example.

Hardware	35%
Software	15%
Contracts and services	10%
Professional development	20%
Support and maintenance	10%
Upgrades and other needs	10%

One of the first steps in this process will be data collection and needs assessment. In this phase of the process the technology coordinator, usually working with the planning committee, will gather such data as inventory and staff development statistics, as well as any other information that provides a current picture of technology in the district. It's also useful to review the technology plan concurrently to see what progress has been made and how the plan is proceeding. In addition, it will be important to communicate with district and building administration, curriculum committees, and other constituencies to identify perceived technology needs and wants throughout the district.

When data has been collected and a list of needs determined, the actual work on a preliminary budget can begin. The budget must be developed to provide resources in two general areas: an operations budget, which provides the funding to pay the ongoing costs of providing technology services and support, and the capital improvements budget, which will provide the funds to purchase new technology resources and provide upgrades and improvements to existing ones.

Specifically, operations funding includes the funds necessary to pay technology staff, provide Internet services, pay contract costs for support agreements and software licensing, purchase day-to-day repair parts, and provide staff development services. Capital costs are those associated with the purchase of new computers, servers, network equipment, replacement and upgrades to workstations, and such other hardware purchases as printers or projectors.

At this point in the process, the technology coordinator will work with technology staff, administration, and other groups to identify specific areas of need. The coordinator will attempt to fit these needs into a workable budget plan. Part of the budget will be made up of fixed costs that will be ongoing and must be factored in first. Fixed costs include such things as salaries, network connectivity, and support contracts. Part of the budget will likely be devoted to equipment replacement and upgrades because machines eventually wear out and must be replaced. The final part of the budget will likely be made up of new initiatives that may be defined by the technology plan or advocated for by the administration, or there may be an initiative suggested by a building or group advocating the implementation of something new. It's the responsibility of the tech coordinator to create a workable first draft of the budget by successfully balancing the specified needs and their costs.

Once the first draft of the budget has been developed, the budget will usually be submitted to central administration for consideration. During the time all departments and units of the school district are in the process of developing draft budget proposals, a period of negotiation and revision will begin to take place. The technology coordinator will need to work with central administration to help them understand the various elements that went into the draft budget proposal, including the needs outlined in the technology plans, targeted in the needs assessment, and expressed by the staff of schools or departments.

As budget negotiations continue, the technology budget, along with all other departmental and school budgets, will go through a process of revision. During this period, considerable give and take must take place. Each department will have identified needs, wants, and goals for their budget. Their draft budgets will reflect these different goals, and there will be some level of competition for budget funding. The district must find a way through negotiation and compromise to successfully balance the needs of all the departments while dealing with the realities of a limited budget. Given the current condition of the economy in most states and communities, few school boards are willing to levy increased taxes in order to increase school budgets.

Following the negotiations with central administration and other departments, the final draft of the technology budget will be developed. The actual budget will be set by the local board of education, so it's important for the technology coordinator to be able to justify the budget as presented and base the budget requests on data that can show the benefits of technology spending for the district. By beginning early, using data to determine need, developing a draft budget based on realistic expectations, considering the needs of others, and being willing to compromise, the tech coordinator can ensure that a successful technology budget is developed for the district.

Evaluation

Schools have invested large sums to implement educational technology in classrooms. While it's been acceptable, up to now, to evaluate this investment either in terms of numbers of students per computer or level of Internet connectivity, school leaders increasingly must find ways to determine if this investment is paying off in terms of student learning. With the growing emphasis on school accountability, the ability to demonstrate the beneficial impact of educational technology has never been more important for schools. The development of assessment tools and techniques that will reliably evaluate the effective use of technology in classrooms and staff rooms is a considerable challenge for the technology coordinator. This process is crucial for demonstrating that the technology program is on track, and that modifications to the program are being made as necessary to better serve the needs of students, teachers, and staff.

As with any other part of the educational program, technology evaluation must be a systematic process. The technology coordinator must begin by identifying how the evaluation will be structured and what's to be learned from it. Assessment tools should be selected or developed based on the fundamental goals of the school's or district's technology plan. They may include surveys, interviews, observations, focus groups, checklists, paper and pencil or online instruments, and analysis of additional data such as standardized test scores or scores from state or local assessments. Many resources on technology evaluation and assessment can be found on the Internet. See the resources section at the end of this chapter for several useful tools.

Once data have been collected from either existing sources or new assessments, the information must be analyzed in order to draw conclusions and make judgments about the program. The data collected during this process can be important in making long-range decisions about future technology purchases and initiatives. Assessment must be an ongoing process, of course, since technology and the way users employ it are always changing. The evaluation process will need to be continuously revised, modified, and adapted to successfully gauge performance and growth.

Assessment results should be shared with a variety of different audiences—the administration, the board of education, and the community—tailoring the information to the particular needs of each of these groups to help them understand the importance of technology investment and the ways in which students are benefiting from this investment. Visual representations such as graphs and charts, for example, can be far more effective with a community group or the local board of education than can a long, detailed report or narrative. On the other hand, state departments of education may require a detailed narrative with plenty of data. It's important to carefully consider the intended audience when planning this assessment report.

helpful hint

Branzburg Procedures

Branzburg (2001) offers a useful step-by-step list of procedures to consider when planning technology assessment:

- Discuss why you are evaluating.
- Determine specific questions you want to answer.
- Decide what data will help to answer your questions.
- Design the evaluation. Get help if necessary.
- Collect the data.
- Analyze the information collected.
- Share your results with others.
- Use the information to make effective decisions.

Meaningful technology assessment can offer a variety of benefits. Results from the assessment will help demonstrate whether the technology program is making progress, the investment has been worthwhile, and adjustments in the way the program is operating are necessary. The conversations that result from planning and implementing the assessment will also help everyone involved to better understand the program and its focus. By offering leadership in this process, initiating the conversations, working with administrators and teachers to design or select assessments, and helping analyze and share the results, the technology coordinator can play a critical role in the continuous improvement of the school's or district's technology program.

Grants

Grants have become a regular part of the funding equation for educational technology leaders. While they shouldn't be viewed as a routine component of the regular technology budget, they can provide useful dollars for exploring new technologies, funding innovative projects, and enhancing professional development opportunities. Grant applications often require considerable time and intense work and commitment from the technology coordinator, but they can also provide welcome additional resources.

Two basic types of grants are available to schools: entitlement grants and competitive grants. Entitlement grants are those funds allocated to schools and districts primarily on the basis of a formula. The formula is intended to distribute the available funds to districts based on an equitable funding method. Funding of entitlement grants is not competitive but is based on eligible student count and other data.

Examples of entitlement grants would include Title I, Title VI, or Eisenhower funds. The purpose of entitlement grants is to provide funding to state and local educational agencies to help them implement educational programs. Entitlement grants provide funds mandated by law. Local educational agencies set up entitlement grant programs based on the criteria of the entitlement program. Appropriations are usually determined by formulas based on enrollment, high concentrations of low-income families, and other needs factors. To receive entitlement funding from a state or federal agency, local school districts must report a variety of data about their student population, for example, enrollment, participation in the free and reduced-fee lunch program, and so forth.

Competitive grants are programs in which the applicant designs a project that competes with other applications for funding. The agency that sponsors the grant program selects projects and determines grant amounts based on preestablished selection criteria. Some competitive grant programs are funded by state or federal education agencies. The other source for competitive grant funds are programs sponsored by private foundations or businesses. While entitlement grants are usually based on financial need, competitive grants are most often awarded based on specific criteria specified by the funding source. Most competitive grant applications will be evaluated on issues such as potential benefit to the students, how well the project addresses an educational need, and the integrity of the project's objectives, planning, and budget.

While each grant is different, most grants tend to be made up of the same basic components: an executive summary, a statement of needs, the project's goals and objectives, a project narrative, and a budget for the project. The executive summary provides a clear overview of the project in a concise format. The statement of needs details the compelling reason for the project. The goals lay out the project's intended results. The objectives suggest ways to evaluate the success of the project. The project narrative provides a specific plan for what will happen and when. The project budget clearly explains, in concise terms, how the funding for the project will be spent.

helpful hint

Grant Writing

Solomon (2001) provides some very useful pointers on things to do before you begin writing a grant:

- *Have a solid idea and plenty of supporting details.*

- *Read the guidelines carefully and make sure the grant fits your needs.*

- *Involve others to build commitment to the project so that there is plenty of support to carry out the project if funded.*

- *Make sure the funding will be sufficient for the project; look for matching funds from other sources if necessary.*

- *Make sure you have the commitment from administration to carry out the project.*

- *Read all the directions and follow them carefully.*

Successful grant writing requires that the technology coordinator come up with a workable idea that fits the grant criteria, provide a project outline that will persuade the grant reader of the value of this idea, and list enough details to make it clear the project is doable.

As mentioned, developing successful grant applications is a time-consuming process. The first step is developing a grant concept that meets the criteria of the grant and is based on a need of the organization. Data must be gathered to support this need and provide information about how the grant project will support the need. When developing the grant concept, it's important to communicate with, and gather support from, district staff and administration to ensure it will be possible to carry out the project. A funded project may be based on an outstanding concept, but if the staff and administration don't support the project, it will have little chance of being successful.

Once a grant concept has been selected and support for the project assured, the actual writing of the proposal can begin. A proposal usually starts with an executive summary, which is a brief summary of the entire grant proposal that gives the reader a general understanding of the project. As a first look, it provides information on the problem to be addressed, a summary of the project and how it will deal with the problem, and a summary of the funding requirements of the project. The executive summary is the part of the proposal that gets a grant reader's attention and creates interest in the project.

The executive summary is followed by a detailed statement of need. This statement provides the facts and figures that support the need, and it helps the reader understand the issues involved. This statement also ties the identified need to the mission and goals of the organization; for example, if the grant is intended to strengthen the use of technology in the learning process it shows how the grant would support the district goals of integrating technology in instruction. While the statement of need must provide background and tie the project to the solution, it does not have to be long. Concise and persuasive writing will be more effective than will a long and involved narrative.

The next section of the proposal is the project description. This section will usually include four subsections: objectives, methods, staffing/administration, and evaluation. Objectives are the measurable outcomes of the program. Your objectives must be specific, measurable, and achievable in a specified time period. The methods section describes the specific activities that will take place to achieve the objectives. You will need to devote a few sentences to discussing the number of staff, their qualifications, and specific assignments. An evaluation plan should not be considered only after the project is over; it should be built into the project. Including an evaluation plan in your proposal indicates that you take your objectives seriously and want to know how well you have achieved them.

Finally, a budget for the project must be prepared. The budget for your proposal may be as simple as a one-page statement of projected expenses or may require a more complex presentation. The budget is intended to help both you and the funding source understand how the money will be spent.

For most projects, costs should be grouped into subcategories, selected to reflect the critical areas of expense. You might divide your expense budget into personnel and nonpersonnel costs. Your personnel subcategories might include salaries, benefits, and consultants. Subcategories under nonpersonnel costs might include travel, equipment, and printing, with a dollar figure attached to each line.

Grants are all about meeting the needs of the organization: "Money by itself is not the answer; it is important to remember that you're there to meet the needs of the school" (Coburn, 1999). By taking the time to explore grant funding opportunities, working with others to develop the support needed to carry out a grant project, and crafting a winning grant application, the technology coordinator can secure the funding necessary to carry out a meaningful technology project.

E-rate Applications

Locating adequate funding to support a technology program is always a challenge for schools and districts. Technology coordinators can help bridge funding gaps by participating in the E-rate program, which was established by the Federal Communications Commission and made available through the Schools and Libraries Division (SLD) of the Universal Service Administrative Company.

The E-rate program was established as part of the Telecommunications Act of 1996 to improve telecommunications services in schools, libraries, and hospitals. By participating in this program, the technology coordinator can help the school or district improve its telephone and Internet connectivity, purchase computers and software, and provide additional training for teachers and staff.

The E-rate program bridges funding gaps by offering schools discounts of 20% to 90% for telecommunications services they purchase or improvements they make to their network infrastructure. All schools can participate in the program by developing a technology plan, determining what services they currently use or wish to acquire, soliciting any necessary bids for those services, and awarding contracts based on the bids.

The technology coordinator begins the E-rate funding process by filing Form 470, providing the description of services and improvements required. The number of free and reduced-fee lunches served by the school or district determines the amount of the discount. Those districts serving students with greater levels of need receive the highest discounts. Bids must be solicited to determine the actual cost of these services and improvements.

After bids have been solicited, final negotiations completed, and agreements made, the technology coordinator takes the second formal step in the process: filing Form 471, Services Ordered Confirmation form. This form describes the actual costs of the services selected, determines the level of discount available to the district, and formally completes the first phase of the E-rate application. Form 471 must be filed according to the deadline determined annually by the SLD.

When the E-rate filing deadline has passed, the Schools and Libraries Division processes all Form 471 applications, determines the amount of funds requested across the nation, verifies applications, and decides the E-rate awards for each applicant. All schools that apply within the eligibility window qualify for discounts on telecommunications services, such as basic telephone service, long-distance charges, and Internet access. Once these services have been provided to all applicants, any remaining funds will be distributed to schools for network infrastructure improvements, which are referred to as internal connections, beginning with those schools in greatest need.

Some recent changes have been implemented by the Schools and Libraries Division when considering applications for internal connections. Starting in funding year 2005, eligible entities will be able to receive support for internal connections in only two out of every five funding years. The five-year period begins in any year in which that entity receives support for internal connections. This limitation does not apply to telecommunications and Internet access services.

All schools can benefit from the discounts on telecommunications services and Internet access. These services alone can total thousands of dollars for a school or district, and the discounts can allow technology coordinators to allocate additional funds to other technology projects.

When final decisions have been made on the discounts available to a district, an official Funding Commitment Decision letter will be issued. This letter identifies the level of discount and the amount of funding available from each service provider identified on Form 471. Following the receipt of the funding letter, the district must file a Form 486, which acknowledges the receipt of services from the vendor and allows the district to officially begin receiving discounts or rebates on services.

In order to begin receiving the actual discounts on services, the district will need to work with service providers to determine the most appropriate method of receipt. Discounts may automatically be applied to monthly bills for services or received as a cash rebate. To receive cash payments, the district must, in conjunction with the service provider, complete Form 472, the Billed Entity Applicant Reimbursement form. This form identifies services received from a vendor and paid for in full. Filing a BEAR form notifies the Schools and Libraries Division to issue a rebate to the vendor. The rebate will be passed on to the district in the form of a check.

While direct discount billing may be simpler for both the district and vendor, there may be situations in which the receipt of a rebate check will be more appropriate and desirable. The technology coordinator should work with administration, business officials, and service providers to determine which method is most convenient and advantageous.

E-RATE SUCCESS

Following are 10 tips for success with the E-rate program application process:

1 Begin thinking about E-rate early. Deadlines always arrive at busy times, and the application process can take longer than expected.

2 Spend time researching the current cost of services used by the district. This may help identify new areas in which to apply for E-rate funding.

3 Be familiar with the products and services eligible for discount.

4 When in doubt about something related to the E-rate process, call the SLD Program Assistance Hotline for help, 1-888-203-8100, or visit their Web site for assistance, **www.sl.universalservice.org.**

5 Be sure to read directions carefully, fill in all required blanks on forms, and file forms by the deadlines.

6 Include E-rate in the technology planning process to ensure compliance with all program requirements and certifications.

7 Keep copies of all forms submitted in case they're needed for reference or program audit.

8 If you disagree with a funding decision, file an appeal. It will take time for a decision, but there will be no penalty and the results may be to your advantage.

9 If necessary, hire an E-rate consultant. These consultants offer management services and provide help with paperwork. They charge 5% to 8% of the discounts received and will take care of the entire application process. It's important to note that vendors of E-rate-services should not be allowed to complete E-rate forms and other paperwork for a district. Such action is prohibited by SLD rules, and doing so is grounds for disqualification from the program.

10 Always budget fully for any services requested through the E-rate program. Requests can be denied or funding reduced. If sufficient funds have not been budgeted, important services or projects can fail due to lack of funding.

ANSWERS TO
Essential Questions

1 What should the technology coordinator know about developing a comprehensive and successful technology plan?

The technology coordinator must work with administration, staff, and community members to develop a comprehensive plan that will address all aspects of the technology program implemented in the district.

2 How can the technology coordinator assist administrators in creating and carrying out a sound technology budget?

The technology coordinator must work with administrators, curriculum committees, and school constituencies to identify technology needs. Funds must be carefully allocated to support fixed costs, equipment purchases, maintenance and upgrades, and new initiatives.

3 How can the technology coordinator assist in evaluating the effectiveness of technology use in the school or district?

The technology coordinator should be familiar with resources and tools that can be used to assess technology use and integration. It's important to share evaluation results with stakeholders to guide ongoing planning efforts.

4 What does the technology coordinator need to know about grant writing to locate and secure additional funding for technology projects?

By involving a variety of people in the planning process and constructing an effective grant application, the technology coordinator can help locate needed funds for innovative projects.

5 What should the technology coordinator know about the E-rate program and application process?

By understanding the various steps and forms involved in the E-rate application process, the technology coordinator can help the district acquire discounts on products and services that will assist in the support of the district technology program.

Resources

PRINT RESOURCES

Barnett, H. (2001). *Successful K–12 technology planning : Ten essential elements.* (ERIC Digest). Syracuse, NY: ERIC Clearinghouse on Information and Technology. (ERIC Document Reproduction Service No. ED457858)

Branzburg, J. (2001). How well is it working? *Technology and Learning, 21*(7), 24-35.

Coburn, J. (1999). Successful approaches to funding. *Technology and Learning, 19*(6), 54-58.

Espey, L. (2000). *Technology planning and technology integration: A case study.* San Diego, CA: Society of Information Technology and Teacher Education International Conference Proceedings. (ERIC Document Reproduction Service No. ED444467)

Fulton, D. (1998). *E-rate: A resource guide for educators.* Syracuse, NY: ERIC Clearinghouse on Information and Technology. (ERIC Document Reproduction Service No. ED420307)

Heinecke, W., & Blasi, L. (1999). *New directions in the evaluation of the effectiveness of educational technology.* Washington, DC: The Secretary's Conference on Educational Technology Proceedings. (ERIC Document Reproduction Service No. ED452825)

New York State Education Department. (1996). *Guidelines for instructional technology planning and application.* Albany, NY: New York State Education Department Office of Facilities Planning. (ERIC Document Reproduction Service No. ED428510)

Salpeter, J. (2002). Accountability: Meeting the challenge with technology. *Technology and Learning, 22*(6), 20-30.

Solomon, G. (2001). Writing and winning grants. *Technology and Learning, 21*(11), 44-50.

Staihr, B., & Sheaff, K. (2001). *The success of the E-rate in rural America.* Kansas City, MO: Federal Reserve Bank Center for the Study of Rural America. (ERIC Document Reproduction Service No. ED455082)

ONLINE RESOURCES

District Technology Self-Assessment Form: www.fno.org/techsurvey.html

Education Department Technology Grant Programs:
www.ed.gov/about/offices/list/os/technology/edgrants.html

Examples of Educational Technology Surveys from the U.S. Department of Education: An Educator's Guide to Evaluating the Use of Technology in Schools and Classrooms: www.ed.gov/pubs/EdTechGuide/appc.html

How-to Guide for Writing Grant Proposals, Forming Partnerships, and Raising Funds: http://darkwing.uoregon.edu/~moursund/GrantWriting/index.htm

HPR*tec Profiler Online Collaboration Tool (technology surveys available): http://profiler.scrtec.org

Institutionalization of Technology in Schools Checklist:
www.wmich.edu/evalctr/checklists/institutionalization_of_tech.htm

Integration of Technology Observation Instrument:
www.west.asu.edu/pt3/assessment/documents/ASUWObservation.pdf

ISTE/CEO Forum STaR (School Technology and Readiness) Chart Self-Assessment Tool: http://ww2.iste.org/starchart/

ISTE Links to Funding and Grant Writing Resources:
www.iste.org/resources/funding/index.cfm

Mankato Survey of Professional Technology Use, Ability and Accessibility:
www.isd77.k12.mn.us/resources/survey.pdf

National Center for Technology Planning: www.nctp.com

National Educational Technology Standards Project: http://cnets.iste.org

NCREL enGauge is a site designed to help districts and schools plan and evaluate the systemwide use of educational technology: www.ncrel.org/engauge/

NCRTec Guiding Questions for Technology Planning:
www.ncrtec.org/capacity/guidewww/gqhome.htm

North Central Regional Educational Laboratory, Planning and Evaluation Links:
www.ncrtec.org/pe/

North Central Regional Educational Laboratory, Technology in Education Links: www.ncrel.org/sdrs/areas/te0cont.htm

Online Examples of Successful Grant Applications:
www.schoolgrants.org/proposal_samples.htm

Technology Applications Center for Educator Development, Assessment Tool
Links: www.tcet.unt.edu/START/assess/tools.htm

Technology Information Center for Administrative Leadership:
www.portical.org/matrix1.html

USAC Schools and Libraries E-rate Site: www.sl.universalservice.org

U.S. Department of Education, Office of Educational Technology:
www.ed.gov/Technology/index.html

U.S. Department of Education, Grants and Contracts Information:
www.ed.gov/about/offices/list/ocfo/gcsindex.html

Writing and Winning Grants, a Web Tour:
http://techlearning.com/db_area/archives/TL/200106/webtour.html

Evaluation and Assessment Tools

District Technology Self-Assessment Form: www.fno.org/techsurvey.html

U.S. Department of Education, an Educator's Guide to Evaluating the Use of
Technology in Schools and Classrooms (examples of educational technology
surveys): www.ed.gov/pubs/EdTechGuide/appc.html

Institutionalization of Technology in Schools Checklist:
www.wmich.edu/evalctr/checklists/institutionalization_of_tech.htm

Integration of Technology Observation Instrument:
www.west.asu.edu/pt3/assessment/documents/ASUWObservation.pdf

Mankato Survey of Professional Technology Use, Ability, and Accessibility:
www.isd77.k12.mn.us/resources/survey.pdf

NCREL enGauge (a site designed to help districts and schools plan and evaluate
the systemwide use of educational technology): www.ncrel.org/engauge/

HPR*tec Profiler Online Collaboration Tool (technology surveys available):
http://profiler.scrtec.org

Technology Applications Center for Educator Development (offers links to a
variety of assessment tools and resources):
www.tcet.unt.edu/START/assess/tools.htm

glossary

administrative computing. The computing done by an educational organization that includes such business tasks as budgeting, payroll, and purchasing. It also includes tasks such as management of human resources information and the processing of such student data as grades and other student records. These administrative tasks are usually carried out by professional office staff, and they are separate from the educational computing done by teachers and students.

adware. See *spyware.*

archive. A backup set of computer files that have been grouped and usually compressed to make available more storage space on a hard disk.

backup. A copy of files or databases that is placed in storage in case of equipment malfunction or other catastrophe. Backing up computer files is usually a regular part of the operation of servers and mainframe computers.

bid request. A formal or informal proceeding for obtaining the costs of providing specified goods or services. Formal bids are documents containing specifications detailing technical requirements for goods and services. Requests for bids are publicly advertised, and bids must be submitted in a sealed bid package or envelope. Formal bids are opened in public and read aloud.

CD-ROM. A compact disc designed to be read by a computer and intended to store computer data rather than audio music files. Many computers today have special drives that allow the creation of both data and music CD-ROMs.

cloning (a drive image). The copying of a complete hard drive as an image file so that the drive can be copied as a whole onto another computer. Cloning of hard drives makes possible the setting up of a single computer from which clones can be made and then installed on as many other machines as necessary.

CPU. The central processing unit, or "brain," of the computer. This main unit does all the work of the computer and controls all the various systems that make up the computer.

database. A collection of data organized in a standard format for easy access, management, and updating by a computer.

data processing. The conversion of raw data to a standard format that can be used by a computer and the subsequent processing—such as storing, updating, combining, rearranging, or printing—of this data by a computer.

desktop computer. A computer intended for use by a single user and designed so that it can be located on a standard desktop.

document imaging. The conversion of paper-based documents into computerized electronic images. A scanner is used to input documents into the system. The document-imaging system is designed to store images on a hard drive or optical disc for easy access of large amounts of data by one or more users.

drive image. A drive image is a file that's an exact and complete image of an entire hard drive. The image contains information on the disk format and structure, a complete installation of the operating system, directories, and all files. A drive image can be used to make a complete copy of a hard drive on another computer or to restore a hard drive following an equipment failure.

DVD (digital videodisc). An optical disc designed for high-capacity storage that is often used for storage of video data files (such as a movie) or computer data. Computers with DVD-ROM drives and even DVD creation drives are becoming much more common for desktop computer models.

educational technology. A term widely used to describe the use of technology tools and resources in an educational setting. Instructional technology refers to the use of the technology for teaching and learning.

e-mail client. A program running on a desktop computer that allows the user to send, receive, and organize electronic mail. An e-mail client connects to a server-based mail account to check for new messages and send messages to others.

E-rate. A government program that provides discounts to help most schools and libraries in the United States obtain affordable telecommunications and Internet access. This program includes three service categories: telecommunications services, Internet access, and internal connections of equipment. Discounts range from 20% to 90% of the costs of eligible services, depending on the level of financial need and the urban or rural status of the population served. Eligible schools, school districts, and libraries must apply for, and be awarded, the discounts on an annual basis, following the guidelines for the program.

ergonomics. An applied science concerned with the interactions of humans with the elements of a system they use. This includes the principles, data, and methods of design needed to optimize human well-being and overall system performance, particularly in a working or learning environment.

fiber-optic line. See *high-speed communications line.*

help desk. A person or persons in an organization who serve as the first point of contact for users needing assistance and information in order to solve technical problems. Help desks are normally established to provide information-technology support, but they may be designed to support other functions of an organization as well.

high-speed communications line. A T1, T3, or fiber-optic line used for carrying voice or data communications signals. A T1 line can carry 24 digitized voice channels, or it can carry data at a rate of 1.544 megabits per second. A T3 line is a super-high-speed connection capable of transmitting data at a rate of 45 million bits per second. This represents a bandwidth equal to about 672 regular voice-grade telephone lines, which is wide enough to transmit full-motion real-time video, as well as very large databases, over a busy network. A T3 line is typically installed as a major networking artery for large corporations and universities with high-volume network traffic. Fiber-optic connections are essentially glass communications wire. Fiber-optic transmission lines can be used to support 30,000 times the traffic that can be carried on copper wires, which make up T1 or T3 lines.

hub. In network communications, a hub is a place of intersection where data arrives from one or more locations and is forwarded on in one or more directions. Hubs are quickly becoming obsolete as they are replaced by more useful and versatile network switches.

information management. Refers to the various stages of information processing—from creation and production to storage, retrieval and dissemination—that's intended to improve the work flow of an organization. Prior to entering the management system, this information can be from internal and external sources and in a variety of formats.

instructional technology. Refers to hardware (such as personal computers, CD-ROMs, and multimedia, handheld learning devices) and software used in instructional programs. Also included are distance-learning activities, such as the Internet, videos, television, satellite, radio, cable, fiber optics, shortwave, microwave, and other related technologies.

local area network (LAN). A computer network that covers a relatively small area. Most LANs cover a single building or a small group of buildings. A system of LANs can be connected over any distance through telephone lines and radio waves, creating a wide-area network

network. A series of points or nodes interconnected by communication paths. In the case of computer networks, it's a variety of different equipment resources, each having a unique identification and serving a particular purpose, such as server, printer, switch, router, and so forth.

password. A sequence of characters typed during a connection sequence to verify that a computer user requesting access is authorized to use a system. Typically, users of a multi-user-protected single-user system claim a unique name, usually called a user ID. In order to verify that someone entering a user ID really is the person who's claimed that name, a second identification, the password, which is known only to that person and to the system itself, is entered by the user to gain access to the system.

patch panel. A hardware unit containing a set of port locations in a communications or other electronic system. In a network, a patch panel serves as a sort of static switchboard, using cables to connect computers within a local area network (LAN) and also to connect them outside to the Internet or another wide area network (WAN). A patch panel uses a network cable called a patch cord to create each interconnection.

print server. A dedicated electronic server that connects a printer to a network. This device enables users to print independently of the file server or a dedicated PC.

router. On the Internet, a router is an electronic device that determines the next network point to which a packet should be sent on its way toward its destination. The router is connected to at least two networks and decides which way to send each information packet based on its current understanding of the state of the networks it's connected to. A router is located at any gateway (where one network meets another), including each Internet point-of-presence. A router is often included as part of a network switch.

rubric. A scoring tool that lists the criteria for a piece of work, in other words, "what counts." For example, purpose, organization, details, voice, and mechanics are often what count in a piece of writing. A rubric also articulates gradations of quality for each criterion, from excellent to poor. In essence a rubric is an evaluation mechanism for rating the quality of a product based on particular criteria.

server. A specialized computer that's attached to a network and is used to provide the other computers in the network with such services as access to files or shared peripherals, or the routing of e-mail.

site license. A license that gives permission to use a software package on more than one system. Site licenses are a means of providing a bulk rate to companies and schools that want to use software on many computers. Organizations are often able to negotiate special pricing when programs are used widely throughout the organization.

software. A general term for the various kinds of programs used to operate computers and related devices.

spreadsheet. A computer program that simulates a paper-based spreadsheet by capturing, displaying, and manipulating data arranged in rows and columns.

spyware. A technology that gathers information about a person or organization without their knowledge. Spyware usually refers to software that's covertly downloaded into someone's computer to secretly gather information about the user. It can be the relatively harmless gathering of generic information about Web sites visited, or it can be malicious, such as the collecting of passwords. A similar type of program is *adware*, a hidden software program that transmits user information to advertisers via the Internet. Both types of programs use up computer resources and network bandwidth and often cause problems for the computers on which they're running. Considerable time is spent by technical-support staff who must remove this software from users' machines.

staff development. Professional training to improve and advance the knowledge, skills, and effectiveness of teachers for their own benefit and the benefit of their students.

technology plan. A document that represents the very best thinking regarding technology use. In education, this thinking accumulates from a variety of stakeholders in a variety of environments—school buildings, school districts, communities, states, and so forth. Technology planning is used to determine ways in which the curriculum and the learning process can be strengthened through the use of technology, and the technology plan sets forth a detailed course to follow to achieve these goals.

Trojan horse. A program that does something users would not approve of if they knew about it. A virus is a particular type of Trojan horse, namely one that's able to spread to other programs. It's often a destructive program that masquerades as a benign one. For example, the user runs such a program, believing it has a useful function, when in fact it's designed to erase a hard drive.

troubleshooting. The process of systematically locating, diagnosing, and fixing problems concerning machinery, technical equipment, and other resources.

T1 line, T3 line. See *high-speed communications line.*

virus. A program or piece of code that's loaded onto your computer without your knowledge and runs against your wishes. Most viruses can replicate themselves and spread to other computers. All computer viruses are manmade. Anti-virus programs periodically check your computer system for the best-known types of viruses.

Web browser. Computer programs, such as Netscape Navigator, Microsoft Internet Explorer, Mosaic, and Safari, that help you navigate the Web and access text, graphics, hyperlinks, audio, video, and other multimedia. Browsers work by "translating" or "interpreting" hypertext markup language (HTML), the code embedded in Web pages that tells them how to look.

wide area network (WAN). A network that connects several local area networks (LANs) over significant distances. WANs use technologies such as ISDN, frame relay, fiber-optic connections, or T1 leased lines to enable users on different LANs to communicate.

worm. A self-contained computer program able to spread functional copies of itself to other computer systems, usually via network connections. Unlike viruses, worms don't need to attach themselves to a host program in order to do damage.

sample job descriptions

POSITION TITLE

Technology Coordinator

DEPARTMENT

Technology

REPORTS TO

District Director of Grants, Federal Programs, and
Information Services

SUMMARY

Under supervision of the District Director of Grants, Federal
Programs, and Information Services, coordinates district
technology program—including networks, computers, and
audiovisual media—and works as part of the district team to
incorporate technology into the curriculum and instruction of
Grades K–12. The position includes responsibilities such as
working on committees; communicating and coordinating
with disciplines, schools, grade levels, faculty, and staff;
planning, designing, coordinating, and providing training;

planning and facilitating technology equipment and supplies orders and implementing their use. Ensures smooth operation of the district's technology, educational access cable channel, satellite access, and distance learning.

ESSENTIAL DUTIES AND RESPONSIBILITIES

- Designs, oversees, maintains, and upgrades the district's network, components, and servers.
- Recommends, implements, and upgrades the district's network technology plan.
- Ensures regular and remote access to servers and the Internet.
- Implements the computer- and technology-education program of the district.
- Reviews and evaluates new educational and administrative software as it is developed.
- Works with committees to develop technology to meet instructional objectives.
- Coordinates workshops for the district's technology-education program for the public.
- Coordinates distribution of computer software in the schools.
- Serves as a direct resource and consultant for faculty, staff, and students.
- Troubleshoots staff problems with technology and other equipment.
- Participates in development of district policies and procedures.
- Conducts research for the district and assists in disseminating findings.
- Networks with outside experts and imports worthwhile ideas and programs into the district.
- Coordinates follow-up to, and compliance with, state and national norms and mandates.

- Coordinates telecommunication services throughout the district, including television and distance learning.
- Prepares budget requests for technology areas.

Other duties may be assigned.

COORDINATING RESPONSIBILITIES

Will coordinate computer technicians' daily activities.

QUALIFICATION REQUIREMENTS

To perform this job successfully, an individual must be able to perform each essential duty satisfactorily. The requirements listed below are representative of the knowledge, skill, and ability required. Reasonable accommodations may be made to enable individuals with disabilities to perform the essential functions.

EDUCATION AND EXPERIENCE

Bachelor's degree in education, business, or technology. Experience in computer science and technology.

CERTIFICATES, LICENSES, REGISTRATIONS

No certification is required for this position.

job description 2

POSITION TITLE

Coordinator of Technology

POSITION SUMMARY

Provide an advanced level of technical expertise in technology planning, including developing standards and supporting the district's personal computers, local area network, wide area networks, and related technologies. Serve as primary resource for district personnel in analyzing user problems related to computers, data communications, and platforms for current and future needs.

QUALIFICATIONS

Technical Skills Required:

- Bachelor's degree in computer science, or an equivalent combination of education and experience from which comparable knowledge and abilities have been acquired.

- Broad background in installing and supporting Novell networks.

- Experience in troubleshooting, with a thorough understanding of PCs, networks, and data communications.

- Ability to closely track difficult problems, document them, and provide effective solutions.

Personal Skills Required:

- Strong interpersonal and written-communication skills, ability to develop positive working relationships with technical and nontechnical users and to maintain a positive approach when providing service to users, and ability to clearly and precisely document complex technical matters.

- Strong organizational skills and ability to effectively schedule multiple projects or tasks to meet simultaneous deadlines.

- Strong personal initiative and ability to work in a school environment without close supervision. Must be able to maintain positive approach despite conflicting deadlines, shifting priorities, and simultaneous work demands.

RESPONSIBILITIES

Network Management:

- Perform Novell network installations, documentation, and maintenance, such as adding new stations and providing users direct day-to-day assistance in solving network-related problems.

- Plan, implement, and manage wide area network and expansion of that network.

- Maintain and expand CPS connection to Internet through COIN and wide area network.

- Make strategic recommendations regarding network system design and implementation.

- Define network hardware and software requirements and perform network design and implementation.

- Design and aid in implementing data-cabling systems.

Computer Troubleshooting:

- Consult with vendor personnel as part of the problem-determination/problem-resolution cycle.

- Research software problems and consult with vendors regarding resolution.

Acquisition Management:

- Evaluate hardware and software configurations.

- Interface with vendors at a technical level and act as a technical resource for CPS staff members regarding network design and computer hardware.

- Write bid requests and specifications for purchases of new computers and data communications, and evaluate responses.

Education and Consulting:

- Consult with staff on the utilization of telecommunications, computerized information retrieval, and software packages.

- Provide educational services, including on-site training and inservices, that may be required for new and revised hardware and software systems.

Future Planning:

- Research and make recommendations regarding future purchases, providing flexibility and design for technologies of tomorrow.

job description 3

POSITION TITLE

District Computer Coordinator

I. Organizational Relation:

The district computer coordinator is accountable to the district media supervisor but works with the curriculum coordinator, staff-development coordinator, and media specialists to determine work priorities.

II. Primary Function:

To help teachers and media specialists integrate computer skills into the curriculum, and to help teachers obtain, learn, and use computer instructional materials to improve their instructional effectiveness.

III. Responsibilities:

- Inservicing staff on computer skills integration.
- Training media specialists, computer lab aides, and library clerks.
- Previewing and recommending new equipment and software purchases.
- Developing software catalogs and informing staff of software.
- Tracking district software licenses and agreements and advising on building licensing.
- Working with media specialists and principals to help ensure district compliance with computer software copyright laws and policies.
- Working with the District Media Advisory Committee and District Staff Development Committee to develop list of staff technology competencies and inservice program.

IV. Minimum Job Qualifications:

A master of arts degree from an accredited college or university, or the equivalent in educational technology, educational computing, or library media, and five years of successful classroom experience.

V. Time Requirements:

Forty hours per week based on a 10.5-month contract. Hours may be flexible to accommodate inservices held outside the regular school day or school year.

job description 4

POSITION TITLE

Technology Coordinator

Building-Level Technology Coordinator Responsibilities:

- Provide curricular consultation and technical assistance for the integration of technology into all classrooms

- Coordinate technology training programs for entire school community

- Integrate technology into the curriculum

- Promote technology awareness and provide information about technology advancement

- Coordinate the educational application of appropriate computer programs and resources

- Address other topics as identified by a building needs assessment

- Communicate information about outside training opportunities

- Keep personal technological knowledge and skills up-to-date

- Evaluate and select software and hardware

- Protect the integrity and security of the OSDNet resources within the building

- Support district policies related to technology use, including Appropriate Use Guidelines, Internet Code of Conduct, and Use of School District Resources

- Attend technology coordinator meetings

- Communicate with school's Technology Advisory Committee representative

- Inform school staff and administration of district technology developments and policies

- Participate in district-level technology forums

- Support other district technical-support personnel (specifically, the school's tech support specialist) in the successful completion of their duties

- Support implementation of the district's long-range technology plan

- Assist in the evaluation of new forms of technology

- Coordinate the development and maintenance of the school's Web site

- Distribute pertinent technology-related information to staff

- Coordinate and participate in building-level Technology Planning Committee

mini-grant application

application for funding

Deadline for submission:

Time: _____ Date: _____

Return by e-mail attachment to:

Contact Person: _____

_____

PROJECT TITLE:

Name of grant contact: _____

Contact's position:

☐ Teacher ☐ Administrator ☐ Counselor/Other

School: _____

Project start/end dates: _____

ALL PROJECTS MUST BE COMPLETED BY (Date):

_____

Estimated number of student participants: _____

Estimated number of staff participants: _____

Amount requested for this project: _____

Budget:

Itemize your budget according to the following categories and briefly explain your planned spending on the attached spreadsheet template. Return the budget spreadsheet along with your grant application.

1 Salaries and/or stipends (specify to whom and how much)

2 Benefits (must be included for all salaries and stipends; calculate at 12% of salary or stipend)

3 Transportation (list separately for student and faculty transportation)

4 Equipment (must be essential to the project)

5 Supplies (be as specific as possible)

6 Other (child care, other special needs, etc.)

Project goals and objectives:

Project description:
(Be sure to include information on the number of sessions involved and the number of contact hours.)

Describe the products or accomplishments resulting from this project:

Describe how this project will be evaluated:

mini-grant budget

Name: _____

School: _____

Project Title: _____

Category	Item	Description/Explanation	Amount
❶	Salary		
❶	Salary		
❶	Stipend		
❶	Stipend		
		SALARY/STIPEND TOTAL:	
❷	Benefits		
❷	Benefits		
		BENEFITS TOTAL:	
❸	Transportation		
❸	Transportation		
		TRANSPORTATION TOTAL:	
❹	Equipment		
❹	Equipment		
❹	Equipment		
		EQUIPMENT TOTAL:	
❺	Supplies		
❺	Supplies		
		SUPPLIES TOTAL:	
❻	Other		
❻	Other		
		OTHER TOTAL:	
❼	Travel		
❼	Travel		
		TRAVEL TOTAL:	
		TOTAL BUDGET REQUESTED:	

bibliography

Anderson, R., & Dexter, S. (2000). *School technology leadership: Incidence and impact* (National Survey Report No. 6). Irvine, CA: Center for Research on Information Technology and Organizations. (ERIC Document Reproduction Service No. ED449786)

Barnett, H. (2001). *Successful K–12 technology planning: Ten essential elements* (ERIC Digest). Syracuse, NY: ERIC Clearinghouse on Information and Technology. (ERIC Document Reproduction Service No. ED457858)

Bateman, B. (2001). Maximizing your hardware investment. *Technology and Learning, 22*(3), 10-12.

Bateman, B. (2002). Installation made simple. *Technology and Learning, 22*(8), 46-48.

Baylor, A. L., & Ritchie, D. (2002). What factors facilitate teacher skill, teacher morale, and perceived student learning in technology-using classrooms? *Computers and Education, 39*(4), 395-414.

Branzburg, J. (2001). How well is it working? *Technology and Learning, 21*(7). 24-35.

Brown, R. (1999). *Serving six institutions: A history of administrative computing at the Associated Colleges of Central Kansas.* McPherson, KS: Associated Colleges of Central Kansas. (ERIC Document Reproduction Service No. ED444414)

Bushweller, K. (1996). How mighty is your wizard? *The American School Board Journal, 183*(5), a14-a16.

Byrom, E. (2001). *Factors influencing the effective use of technology for teaching and learning.* Retrieved December 12, 2001, from **www.seirtec.org/publications/lessons.pdf**

Carter, K. (2000). Staffing up for technology support. *Technology and Learning, 20*(8), 26-33.

CEO Forum on Education and Technology. (1997). *From pillars to progress.* Retrieved March 26, 2000, from www.ceoforum.org/reports.cfm?RID=1

Christensen, R. (2001). Wiring the schools: South Dakota does it right. *Tech Trends, 45*(3), 18-20.

Coburn, J. (1999). Successful approaches to funding. *Technology and Learning, 19*(6), 54-58.

Dietrich, D. (2003). How to obtain E-rate funding. *School Business Affairs, 69*(4), 33-34.

Durost, R. A. (1994). Integrating computer technology: Planning, training, and support. *NASSP Bulletin, 78*(1), 49-54.

Earle, R. (2002). The integration of instructional technology into public education: Promises and challenges. *Educational Technology, 41*(1), 5-13.

Espey, L. (2000). *Technology planning and technology integration: A case study.* San Diego, CA: Society of Information Technology and Teacher Education International Conference Proceedings. (ERIC Document Reproduction Service No. ED444467)

Farmer, L. S. (2001). Managing the hard stuff: Technology. *Library Talk, 14*(4), 6-9.

Grohe, B., & Levinson, E. (2002). Managing technology is different. *Converge, 5*(1), 42-43.

Hallman, T. (1995). *Getting everyone into the tent.* Myrtle Beach, SC: Association of Small Computer Users in Education Conference Proceedings. (ERIC Document Reproduction Service No. ED387098)

Hardy, L. (2003). Information, please. *American School Board Journal, 190*(7), 20-22.

Harrington-Leuker, D. (2001). *New networks, old problems: Technology in urban schools.* Washington, DC: Education Writers Association Special Report. (ERIC Document Reproduction Service No. ED456188)

Heinecke, W., & Blasi, L. (1999). *New directions in the evaluation of the effectiveness of educational technology.* Washington, DC: The Secretary's Conference on Educational Technology Proceedings. (ERIC Document Reproduction Service No. ED452825)

Hoffman, B. (1996). Managing the information revolution: Planning the integration of school technology. *NASSP Bulletin, 80*(2), 89-98.

Hoffman, R. (2002). Strategic planning: Lessons learned from a "big-business" district. *Technology and Learning, 22*(10), 26-38.

Holland, L., & Moore-Steward, T. (2000). A different divide: Preparing tech savvy leaders. *Leadership, 30*(1), 6-10.

House, J. (1989). *The impact of personal computing on the educational administration knowledge base.* Washington, DC: Education Writers Association Special Report. (ERIC Document Reproduction Service No. ED456188)

Hovenic, G. (1997). *Log on to the future: One school's success story.* Des Moines, IA: Iowa State Department of Education. (ERIC Document Reproduction Service No. ED419518)

Jensen, D. (2000). Creating technology infrastructures in a rural school district: A partnership approach. In S. DeWees & P. Hammer (Eds.), *Improving rural school facilities* (pp. 57-69). Collected papers presented at the National Working Conference on Improving Rural School Facilities, Kansas City, MO. (ERIC Document Reproduction Service No. ED445859)

Jewell, M. (1999). The art and craft of technology leadership. *Learning and Leading with Technology, 26*(4), 46-47.

Joseph, R., & Reigeluth, C. (2002). Beyond technology integration: The case for technology transformation. *Educational Technology, 42*(4), 9-13.

Kranz, M. (2002). Networking systems and equipment. *School Planning and Management, 41*(5), 32-36.

Maddux, C. (2002). Information technology in education: The critical lack of principled leadership. *Educational Technology, 42*(3), 41-50.

Marcovitz, D. M. (1998). *Supporting technology in schools: The roles of computer coordinators.* Washington, DC: Society for Information Technology and Teacher Education Conference Proceedings. (ERIC Document Reproduction Service No. ED421150)

McClure, P. A., Smith, J. W., & Sitko, T. D. (1997). *The crisis in information technology support: Has our current model reached its limit?* Boulder, CO: Association for Managing and Using Information Resources in Higher Education CAUSE Paper Series No.16. (ERIC Document Reproduction Service No. ED403837)

McGillivray, K. (1999). The tool kit: An innovative approach to technology integration in networked schools. *Learning and Leading with Technology, 26*(5), 45-49.

Moursund, D. (1992). *The technology coordinator.* Eugene, OR: International Society for Technology in Education.

Murray, B. (2001). Tech support: More for less. *Technology and Learning, 22*(4), 40-44.

New Mexico State Department of Education. (1995). *Educational technology institute report.* Santa Fe, NM: Author. (ERIC Document Reproduction Service No. ED460673)

New York State Education Department. (1996). *Guidelines for instructional technology planning and application.* Albany, NY: New York State Education Department Office of Facilities Planning. (ERIC Document Reproduction Service No. ED428510)

Palmer, S. (1997). *Leadership styles and problem solving: de Bono's "Six Hats."* Retrieved July 2, 2001, from **www.deakin.edu.au/~spalm/srp70733.html**

Peterman, L., McGillivray, K., & Frantz, J. (1998). Professional development: from reports to reality. *LNT Perspectives.* Retrieved November 11, 2001, from **www.edc.org/LNT/news/Issue6/feature.htm**

Reilly, R. (1999). The technology coordinator: Curriculum leader or electronic janitor? *Multimedia Schools, 6*(3). Retrieved May 24, 2000, from **www.infotoday.com/mmschools/mmstocs/may99toc.htm**

Ritchie, D. (1996). The administrative role in the integration of technology. *NASSP Bulletin, 80*(2), 42-51.

Rodriguez, J. (1997, April). Building an adaptive information system. *AASA School Administrator Web Edition.* Retrieved July 17, 2002, from **www.aasa.org/publications/sa/1997_04/rodriguez.htm**

Rogers, A. (1996). Living in the global village. *Electronic Learning, 13*(8), 28-29.

Salpeter, J. (2002). Accountability: Meeting the challenge with technology. *Technology and Learning, 22*(6), 20-30.

Solomon, G. (2001). Writing and winning grants. *Technology and Learning, 21*(11), 44-50.

Son, T. (1998). *Network technology based application*. Portland, OR: Northwest Regional Educational Lab. (ERIC Document Reproduction Service No. ED417707)

Staihr, B., & Sheaff, K. (2001). *The success of the E-rate in rural America*. Kansas City, MO: Federal Reserve Bank Center for the Study of Rural America. (ERIC Document Reproduction Service No. ED455082)

U.S. Department of Education. (2000a). *e-Learning: Putting a world class education at the fingertips of all children*. Retrieved November 22, 2001, from **www.ed.gov/Technology/elearning/e-learning.pdf**

U.S. Department of Education. (2000b). *Falling through the net: Towards digital inclusion*. Retrieved December 13, 2001, from **http://search.ntia.doc.gov/pdf/fttn00.pdf**

U.S. Department of Education. (2000c). *The power of the Internet for learning*. Retrieved December 20, 2001, from **www.ed.gov/offices/AC/WBEC/FinalReport/**

U.S. Department of Education National Center for Education Statistics. (2000). *Teachers' use of computers and the Internet in public schools*. Retrieved May 20, 2000, from **www.nces.ed.gov/pubsearch/pubsinfo.asp?pubid=2000090**

Wasser, J. (1996). Navigating past the technology on-ramp. *Hands-On! 19*(2). Retrieved November 11, 2001, from **www.terc.edu/handson/f96/navigating.html**

Wasser, J., & McNamara, E. (1998). *Professional development and full school technology integration* (Hanau Model Schools Partnership Research Brief No. 5). Cambridge, MA: TERC.

NETS•A

National Educational Technology Standards for Administrators (NETS•A)

All school administrators should be prepared to meet the following standards and performance indicators. These standards are a national consensus among educational stakeholders regarding what best indicates effective school leadership for comprehensive and appropriate use of technology in schools.

I. Leadership and Vision

Educational leaders inspire a shared vision for comprehensive integration of technology and foster an environment and culture conducive to the realization of that vision. Educational leaders:

A facilitate the shared development by all stakeholders of a vision for technology use and widely communicate that vision.

B maintain an inclusive and cohesive process to develop, implement, and monitor a dynamic, long-range, and systemic technology plan to achieve the vision.

C foster and nurture a culture of responsible risk taking and advocate policies promoting continuous innovation with technology.

D use data in making leadership decisions.

E advocate for research-based effective practices in use of technology.

F advocate, on the state and national levels, for policies, programs, and funding opportunities that support implementation of the district technology plan.

II. Learning and Teaching

Educational leaders ensure that curricular design, instructional strategies, and learning environments integrate appropriate technologies to maximize learning and teaching. Educational leaders:

A identify, use, evaluate, and promote appropriate technologies to enhance and support instruction and standards-based curriculum leading to high levels of student achievement.

B facilitate and support collaborative technology-enriched learning environments conducive to innovation for improved learning.

C provide for learner-centered environments that use technology to meet the individual and diverse needs of learners.

D facilitate the use of technologies to support and enhance instructional methods that develop higher-level thinking, decision-making, and problem-solving skills.

E provide for and ensure that faculty and staff take advantage of quality professional learning opportunities for improved learning and teaching with technology.

III. Productivity and Professional Practice

Educational leaders apply technology to enhance their professional practice and to increase their own productivity and that of others. Educational leaders:

A model the routine, intentional, and effective use of technology.

B employ technology for communication and collaboration among colleagues, staff, parents, students, and the larger community.

C create and participate in learning communities that stimulate, nurture, and support faculty and staff in using technology for improved productivity.

D engage in sustained, job-related professional learning using technology resources.

E maintain awareness of emerging technologies and their potential uses in education.

F use technology to advance organizational improvement.

IV. Support, Management, and Operations

Educational leaders ensure the integration of technology to support productive systems for learning and administration. Educational leaders:

A develop, implement, and monitor policies and guidelines to ensure compatibility of technologies.

B implement and use integrated technology-based management and operations systems.

C allocate financial and human resources to ensure complete and sustained implementation of the technology plan.

D integrate strategic plans, technology plans, and other improvement plans and policies to align efforts and leverage resources.

E implement procedures to drive continuous improvements of technology systems and to support technology-replacement cycles.

V. Assessment and Evaluation

Educational leaders use technology to plan and implement comprehensive systems of effective assessment and evaluation. Educational leaders:

A use multiple methods to assess and evaluate appropriate uses of technology resources for learning, communication, and productivity.

B use technology to collect and analyze data, interpret results, and communicate findings to improve instructional practice and student learning.

C assess staff knowledge, skills, and performance in using technology and use results to facilitate quality professional development and to inform personnel decisions.

D use technology to assess, evaluate, and manage administrative and operational systems.

VI. Social, Legal, and Ethical Issues

Educational leaders understand the social, legal, and ethical issues related to technology and model responsible decision making related to these issues. Educational leaders:

A ensure equity of access to technology resources that enable and empower all learners and educators.

B identify, communicate, model, and enforce social, legal, and ethical practices to promote responsible use of technology.

C promote and enforce privacy, security, and online safety related to the use of technology.

D promote and enforce environmentally safe and healthy practices in the use of technology.

E participate in the development of policies that clearly enforce copyright law and assign ownership of intellectual property developed with district resources.

This material was originally produced as a project of the Technology Standards for School Administrators Collaborative.